MODERN SPEARFISHING

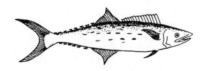

Modern
Spearfishing

VANE IVANOVIĆ

Henry Regnery Company · Chicago

Library of Congress Cataloging in Publication Data

Ivanović, Vane
    Modern spearfishing.

    1. Spear fishing.   I. Title.
GV840.S7819   1975   799.1'4   74-30112
ISBN 0-8092-8269-0
ISBN 0-8092-8268-2 pbk.

CONTENTS

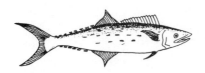

{

*I dedicate this revised version
of my book to my dear friend Eric
Weinmann, companion under the sea
for two decades.*

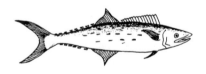

PREFACE

I wrote my first book on spearfishing in 1950.

It was not the first book in the English language describing the sensations experienced in donning a mask and viewing what goes on under the surface of the sea, a lake or river. Just before World War II an American, Guy Gilpatrick, wrote a short book called 'The Compleat Goggler'. He used a pair of simple goggles with two small plates, one over each eye, with his nose uncovered. Americans have ever since used the word 'goggling' for the pastime of floating on the surface and looking at the scene below. For the sport of diving below the surface, with whatever intent, they have used the word 'skin-diving', sometimes spelt 'skindiving'. For all activities using compressed air or oxygen re-breathing apparatus, for dives longer than can be made with one lungful, they use the expression SCUBA (or Scuba diving). This has been obtained, in echo of prevailing *mores* above the water, by shortening the words Self-Contained Underwater Breathing Apparatus.

I have long ago given up protesting against all three of these ghastly additions to the English language. 'Goggles' are no longer in use; therefore no 'goggling': skin-diving could easily mean diving for skins (whatever *that* may mean) and in any case many people now dive in rubber or neoprene suits: 'Scuba diving' is a phrase I cannot comment on in what are still generally accepted as printable words. But, the least I can do here is to avoid these horrors.

This, the second revised edition to my original book, is still devoted to helping those who want to fish under water. They use spears, whatever the method of propulsion. So this book retains its name, 'Modern Spearfishing', to separate this sport from ancient hunting of fish from land or boat by bow and arrow or some form of trident.

I have now made several journeys round the world for the express purpose of gaining experience of spearfishing conditions in seas other than the Mediterranean. I have spearfished off the coasts of Ceylon, Singapore, Thailand, Bali, Hong Kong, Japan and Malaya, Western and South Australia, the Hawaiian Islands, Tahiti, California, Mexico, Puerto Rico, Jamaica, Haiti, Anguilla, Barbados, Grenada, Venezuela, Ecuador, the Virgin Islands and Madeira. I have spearfished off Madagascar and Zanzibar, in the Red Sea and the Persian Gulf. I have been to the Bahamas and to Bermuda many times.

I have now met most of the world's famous spearfishing pioneers and I have seen some of these great men in action: Rodney Jonklaas in Ceylon; Jack Ackerman of Hawaii; Frank Rodecker, whose home is at Hermosa Beach near Los Angeles; General Greatsinger Farrell off the Coronado Islands near the American-Mexican border; Jack Prodanovich, President of the famous 'Bottom Scratchers Club' of San Diego, California; José Beltrán, the great Majorcan spearfisherman; Ross Doe of Bermuda; Charles Chaplin of the Bahamas, the renowned ichthyologist, and Whitney Straight, with whom I spearfished for many years near Formentor Point on Majorca. The most famous men in this world under the sea, Jacques-Yves Cousteau, Dr Hans Hass and Stanton Waterman I knew in the early days. Of the world's greatest spearfishermen, the Italians, I have only seen Ruggero Jannuzzi in action. Dr Eugenie Clark, the famous Lady with a Spear, I have long admired but only lately known.

I hope I have succeeded in conveying some of the knowledge gained in watching these men and woman in action in the form of practical advice to the novice. Their ways represent a great advance over the early efforts of Man to accustom himself to prolonged activity under water.

Spearfishing is now an established sport. The full testing, however, of Man's skill and natural gifts has not yet come. Too many of us, who claim to have acquired some skill at this new sport, spend our time hunting the kind of fish that really correspond to rabbits on land. The novelty has not yet worn off. I had hoped that my original book might have persuaded spearfishermen that in modern spearfishing there was no place for those who were not prepared to run some risks in pursuing the sport of stalking fish in their own element. My first book aspired to be in this sense a Book of Etiquette for the world under water. Now that I am sixty, and still active under water after 36 years, I am harder on etiquette, tougher on vandals, more critical of indiscriminate slaughter and, above all, angry at pollution.

The risks are all given what I hope may be considered a fair account. I have not the ability, not being a poet, to give an adequate picture of the beauty or the nature of the world below water. We have only begun meeting fish as live creatures. We are as ignorant of them and their surroundings as they must be puzzled by the appearance of the grotesque twin-tailed fish whose brief visits so often end in death or pillage.

All I have attempted to do is to give the novice an idea of the most modern methods and weapons of spearfishing, brief notes on some fishes and some elementary things about diving with compressed-air apparatus.

I wish to record my thanks to Dr Gilbert Doukan. The sketches showing various types of sea bed were inspired by his original sketches in *La Chasse Sous-Marine* published in Paris in the early days. The sea beds seem to have remained the same as when I first saw them and so have my sketches from the earlier editions of this book.

I am fortunate enough to be able to reproduce in this book colour and black and white photographs by Roberto Dei, one of Italy's (and therefore the world's) greatest photographers of the world under water, through the help of Franco Capodarte, Editor and most suitably named Head of the Art Department of the world's foremost magazine of the underwater world *Mondo Sommerso*.

I thank the *New Yorker Magazine* and *Punch* for permission to reproduce cartoons published by them.

The photographs of my special underwater fishing boat 'Taro' were made by Messrs John I. Thorneycroft & Co Ltd of England who built it in 1957.

The illustrations of equipment, the fishes and some diving techniques were drawn by Bert Gerry.

I am indebted to Patricia Frost for her infinite patience with the manuscript, and her skill in collating all the new material added in this revision, activities rather far removed from her normal work in a ship-owning company and for the Consulate General of Monaco in London. Penelope Pearson did much of the technical parts of the typing and I render thanks.

I record with gratitude the knowledge I have gained from studying Dr Bruce W. Halstead's monumental work, *Poisonous and venomous marine animals of the world,* a work sponsored by the US Department of Defense.

The prejudices and judgements in this book are mine alone. Even so, I owe much to my many fellow divers all over the world but more than to any occasional companions to my most constant and reliable friends and critics under water, Eric Weinmann, Whitney Straight, Jack Heinz, Neil McLean, Peter Mond, the late Jean Claeyssens, and my two sons and daughter. I have not yet been criticized by my grandchildren but I leave this for the revised edition of this book in 1990 A.D.

Lately, such distinguished men as Jacques-Yves Cousteau and Hans Hass, as well as Stanton Waterman and others, have added their view against spearfishing, or at least against spearing fish with mechanically-propelled weapons.

I have long held the view that spearfishing with an Aqualung was too easy and destructive. In the last edition of this book, published almost twenty years ago, I advised voluntary restraint by the ordinary spearfisherman and roundly condemned spearfishing competitions as irrelevant, unfair and unwise.

Yet, I feel some sense of proportion must be observed. In the time it takes to read these lines several million fish will have been caught all over the world by professional fishermen with the aid of electronic and depth-sounding equipment, very sophisticated netting and the like. In the same space of minutes, all over the world, at most a mere several dozen fish will have been speared by men stalking fish under water. Who is doing damage to the balance of nature? How is the ecological system being disturbed?

In the Chapter entitled 'Perils and Morals' I have said something on this subject. If we pursue voluntary restraint as to the weapons we use and the amount of fish we spear we cannot be condemned for damaging the present natural balances under water. Far more guilty are the professional net fishermen everywhere and the general public that wishes to eat fish or use processed fish in other ways.

1

AMPHIBIAN MAN

He goes a great Voyage, that goes to the bottom of the Sea. THOMAS FULLER
Gnomologia, 1632 A.D. No. 1850

Man let many centuries go by before he took any interest in the world below the sea other than in catching fish. Even this was half-hearted in comparison with his other activities. He merely extracted fish from the Oceans.

Only very recently did he begin to meet with any success in stalking fish under water. The modern way of spearing fish is now about forty years old. Only a few spearfishermen can claim to have swum under water before World War II. Most of these hail from the shores of the Mediterranean, where so many other of Man's undertakings, good and bad, have had their beginnings.

To follow the story of Man's efforts to become amphibian we must follow fishing Man and to some extent fighting Man.

Very probably many thousands of years ago, Man found that some of the weapons used in the pursuit of animals on land could also be used in the water. A sharp stone or bone secured to a wood pole could be used to spear fish in shallow pools near the shore. In time the weapons were gradually made more efficient for use in fishing. The primitive hunting spear, which by then was made of metal, has survived most successfully the test of constant use. In the course of experience it became armed with one or two barbs. Later, the number of points was increased and Neptune, or Poseidon, as the Greeks called the god of the sea, is usually pictured carrying a trident.

In his book *Fishing in Many Waters* (Cambridge University Press) Mr James Hornell has written a fascinating chapter on the weapons of the chase borrowed by fishermen. It is reasonably safe to say that the methods he describes by which Polynesian natives harpoon fish from coral reefs go back to the earliest years of Man's sojourn on Earth. Andaman islanders shoot fish with bow and arrow to this day. When I was a child in Jugoslavia we used to go out on moonless nights with a lantern fixed to the bows of our row boat, and harpoon mesmerized morays, lobsters and octopuses in the shallow waters of our rocky coast.

Variations of fishing spears have been without number, but until recent times Man has remained with his head and hands out of the water. He could not see well enough under water to aim at a moving target, and he could not move his arm quickly enough to pierce a fish with his weapon even if he did manage to get close enough.

History records several spectacular occasions on which Man overcame the problems which arise when by chance he is engulfed by great seas. Noah built an ark, while Moses and the Israelites were fortunate enough to see the Red Sea part for them. Until the advent of the submarine, Jonah held the record for the longest stay below the water.

So far as I have been able to establish, that versatile genius Aristotle was the first to record some coherent and practical thoughts on breathing and the problems which Man would face if he were to stay under water. He thought that it should be possible for Man, when fully immersed, to do what an elephant could do. Aristotle himself may well have lain under water off an Hellenic beach with a short tube in his mouth and stared about him wondering what to do next. He could not have used a tube more than a metre long, because his lungs would not have been strong enough to suck in enough air at a greater depth.

Alexander the Great and the Romans made diving bells. When the bells were immersed and held down in shallow water by great stones, there was enough air for men to sally forth, act and return to take another breath.

There is no recorded evidence of further thought on this problem until just about the time of the Renaissance. This may be due to the overrunning of the civilized world by barbarians (Latin for land-lubbers) after the fall of Rome.

In the writings of a countryman of mine I have come across a sketch apparently dated 1430 A.D. which I reproduce here. I

Fifteenth-century diver working just below the surface

imagine the diver's clothes were made of leather. The diving helmet also is either of leather or possibly the bladder of some large animal. The two dumbbells holding the end of the breathing tube above the surface are probably of cork or wood. Dried gourds would have been just as useful. The stone and anchor on the diver's right help to keep him below the surface, and the barrel tied to the rope in his left hand is presumably for oysters or sponges. The diver seems very surprised at what he saw. I am rather surprised at the suggestion that he saw at all, because if the sketch is a true reproduction of the gear, it means that successful underwater goggles were definitely known in the fifteenth century. The glasses must have been fitted into the diving helmet much in the way that pieces of stained glass were held together to make windows. Without having air at pressure pumped down to him he could not have gone deep.

Mr James M. Osborn of Yale University has come across the works of Rabbards, the English explorer of the fifteenth century. There is evidence of diving gear having been made in England at that time by Rabbards.

The earliest evidence of Man tackling the problem of stalking fish under water is in a book entitled *Submarine Navigation in all Parts of the World* by Commander Delpeuch, published in Paris in 1536. There is in this book a sketch of a leather mask, apparently well-sealed and connected by a tube to a bladder floating on the surface. The illustration also shows a diver holding a fish in his left hand and a spear in the other. He was evidently a much better shot than I am, or than any of the fishermen I have met. I could not see any trace of a window in his mask.

It was inevitable that Leonardo da Vinci (1452–1519) should have turned his great mind to the designing of apparatus for breathing under water. I reproduce a sketch of his, showing what seems to be a tube of bamboo wood or possibly sugar cane, with a wood or cork float.

All these early efforts were doomed to failure and we now know that, owing to tremendously increasing pressure as a human being goes down, only mechanical means of providing air at corresponding pressure can keep a man alive for more than one breath.

Towards the end of the last century Man began to solve some of the problems of staying below the surface longer than the minute or so possible with one breath. Diving helmets and suits

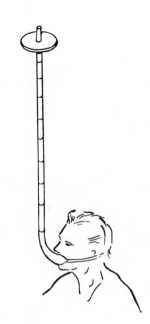

Leonardo's diver

were developed, and much thinking began on the subject of underwater pressure on the diving suit and the body inside it. Submarines
were developed, but still Man was not free under water the way a
fish was.

The first development which paved the way to this freedom was
the goggle.

While in Japan, I tried to pin Japanese pearl divers down to a
date when they first used bamboo or rubber goggles under water.
I was assured that goggles had been in use for many decades, but
could find no evidence of earlier diving masks.

Mr Renzo Avanzo, the famous Italian spearfisherman and frogman instructor, has told me of a brief visit by two mysterious
Japanese 'gogglers' to Capri in 1911. But apart from this occasion
the first that Europe saw of the use of goggles under water was
when some Japanese visitors to the Great Exhibition in Barcelona
in 1930 showed the Catalans that their rough coast was much more
beautiful than they had hitherto believed.

Modern spearfishing was properly born in France, following
upon a visit by Guy Gilpatrick in about 1936, and quickly spread
to other parts of the Mediterranean. Better and more efficient

goggles were rapidly developed, and at last Man had an un-obstructed, clear and comfortable view of the world under water. Rubber fins were probably invented by Owen Churchill and I first came upon them in 1940. They gave new power to Man's legs and feet. With fins any average swimmer could move as fast as Weissmuller did with his bare feet. It was found that when he was totally immersed and away from friction at the surface where water meets the air, Man could move very quickly in all directions.

Man was able to see clearly and move quickly under water. He discovered a world of unsuspected beauty in the sea, and soon developed weapons and breathing apparatus that enabled him to make entirely new tests of his skill, endurance and bravery. A new sport was developed and has taken its place among Man's older pastimes.

Then the snorkel was invented. This is a tube held in the mouth and fitted to the original goggle, so that a swimmer may keep his face under water and swim without pausing for breath or turning his face to breathe. Later the single plate mask, enveloping the nose and eyes, was developed. No water penetrated the nose in dives more than a few centimetres deep, and by snorting into the mask the swimmer could equalize the pressure inside the mask with the water outside.

Finally came the great and revolutionary development during World War II. Captain Jacques-Yves Cousteau of the French Navy and Emile Gagnan developed, from the earlier models pioneered by French Navy Commander Le Prieur and the French Navy under-water department, the first independent breathing apparatus. With a cylinder of compressed air on his back, Man could now spend up to an hour below the surface, living like a fish for this brief time.

At last Man could swim below the water. For centuries he knew how to jump off a cliff, but only learned to fly from the Wright Brothers. For centuries he knew how to float and move about on the surface of the water, but from Cousteau and Gagnan he really learned how to swim like a fish.

The waters around the United Kingdom are not really suitable for beginners at spearfishing. As far as people living in Britain are concerned, this book is intended as a guide for those who have an opportunity of going abroad. Spearfishing and skiing present similar problems and similar solutions. People can prepare for both sports and keep fit at home and enjoy themselves abroad.

The waters of the United States north of Cape Hatteras in the Atlantic and north of Los Angeles in the Pacific are also not suitable for beginners at spearfishing; they are too cold unless rubber or neoprene suits are worn. The American beginner is advised to seek warm waters first. California now boasts thousands of spearfishermen south of Los Angeles, and Florida has become a great centre too. But to Americans the problems of transport are not as forbidding as they are to others. No people on earth move about their own country as much as Americans do. American trips to visit neighbours are often much longer than expeditions abroad are to us in Europe. When I write in this book of Caribbean reefs and tropical fish, I do not have the feeling that I am writing of matters beyond the reach of the average adventurous young American. Once beyond the novice stage, the young American will find good sport all over his country too, provided he is willing to face cooler seas and the mysterious and eerie depths of his inland lakes.

I limit myself to spearfishing in this book because it is the only activity under water of which I have some knowledge.

But the world under water is a vast field for new human experience. Even though the deep oceans may be deserts both on the surface and at the bottom many miles below, the shelf of each Continent is a vast area in which Man's intelligence, courage and ambition may be tested. We can now reach it and we may find it more profitable to explore this world before we get too involved in outer space.

2

FISHING GROUNDS

Litus ama; . . . altum alii teneant. (Hug the shore,
let others keep to the deep.) VIRGIL
Aeneid, Bk v, 1. 163, 19 B.C.

The best fish swim near the bottom. (English
proverb)

It will not profit you much to try spearfishing on the high seas.
If you do manage to see a fish it will probably be too large or too
fast for you. In Chapter 8 you will see that we know nothing about
sharks on the high seas. Our own experience, as spearfishermen,
is only of sharks in the shallow waters and very near the shore,
so that it may be true that Ocean sharks would eat a man on sight.

The great Oceans are in many respects like huge three-dimensional
deserts. Plant-life, coral, molluscs, and all other types of food on
which the smaller fish live, abound only in waters close to the
shore, and not more than thirty fathoms deep where the power of
the sun's rays is still strong. Below these depths the rays from the
sun are gradually absorbed and the inhabitants are strange beings
that we laymen would hesitate to class among ordinary fish
(although sharks have been photographed 1500 metres deep,
about 4000 feet). Only on those highways of the Oceans where
plankton abounds will you find life with which we are familiar.
There are so many factors working against the spearfisherman on
the high seas that I shall not discuss fishing conditions there.

The spearfisherman must search for places where there are small
fish, because this means that sooner or later he will come across
the larger ones who feed on the little ones.

FRESHWATER SPEARFISHING

Rivers are very difficult for the spearfisherman. Clear, swift
mountain streams are usually too shallow for effective diving.
Swimming will only be possible downstream and the diver's whole

attention will be occupied in avoiding stones and whirlpools. Sometimes the depth of water will permit free movement, but this also usually means fast-moving water. The temperature of water in such rivers or torrents will usually be so low that longer exposure will be no pleasure. Even so, some intrepid men have floated down torrents and waterfalls, holding on to bags containing food and camping equipment, thanks to masks, fins and rubber or neoprene suits. Their adventures deserve a book on their own.

In slow rivers, organic matter will impede visibility and many rivers will be full of refuse from industrial plants and nearby cities, making the water dangerous to the naked skin and totally uninteresting except to scientists studying river pollution.

I have yet to hear of attempts to spear salmon as they travel up rivers and I dare say that this sport, if allowed, would provide much fun. Such spearfishing is frowned upon in Canada, so that an important area for experiment is denied us.

Most lakes are very cold too, and experience has shown that the larger fish keep to the depths. When they do come up they spend very little time near the surface. Spearfishing in lakes is a lonely and frustrating pastime, and the men who have done it are the hardy and persistent few, particularly those in the American and Canadian lakes who, in the winter, descend through holes made in the ice.

ESTUARIES, DELTAS, ETC.

The great problem at the mouths of rivers is, again, visibility. Wherever large quantities of fresh water intermingle with salt water you have a tremendous movement of organic matter, mud or sand, and visibility is restricted to, at best, only a few centimetres. And here again you have the problem of cold. However, if you go farther out into the sea, then with every metre you move fishing conditions approach those in salt water.

SALT-WATER FISHING

I start by asserting a general proposition. Spearfishing is possible wherever you can see beyond three metres under water when wearing your mask. The water should be warmer than 13°C (55°F), even when a rubber or neoprene suit is worn. It must be more than 18°C to 22°C (65°F to 70°F) to enable the average swimmer to stay in more than half an hour without wearing protective clothing.

Having established these elementary conditions, there are now further matters to consider. You must try to avoid rough seas, tides and currents, especially if you are a novice. You must try and do your spearfishing away from beaches where you will disturb the bathers who in turn will disturb your fish. You must avoid settlements and ports and places with much traffic on the surface.

Closed seas like the Mediterranean, the Black Sea and the Red Sea have the advantage of not having the large movements of water common in the Oceans.

The tropical seas all around the world are ideal spearfishing grounds. Fish abound, settlements are relatively scarce and the sea is warm. It costs a lot to get to them, however, unless you are a native of some of the beautiful islands of the tropical belts in the Pacific, Atlantic and Indian Oceans.

The beginner will find Southern California, the southern parts of the Atlantic coast of the United States and the Caribbean the most ideal territories. In the Mediterranean, where fishing is an ancient art, there are many beautiful places, but it takes more skill to spear a fish in the Mediterranean than anywhere else, because the fish are scarce and wary.

Suppose you have come to the shore at any one of these places. Make the following analysis of the situation before you begin to fish.

See whether the water is blue up to the very line of the shore. If so, this means that it is likely to be clear, and visibility will be good. If you see discolouration near the shore it may mean that the bottom is sandy or muddy. The slightest movement of water will cause the sand or mud to rise and you will not be able to see.

The next thing to examine is the shore on which you are standing. The kind of sea bottom you encounter will depend on the type of shore next to it.

If there are just rocks, sharpened by tons of sea water being dashed against them daily, it will mean that few plants or corals have been able to survive the great movements of water, and there will be little life immediately below. You will only find more rocks. Though the sea may be crystal clear, most of the quarry you are after will be at greater depths.

If you find large stones above the water, you will find large stones below the surface too.

You may be standing on hilly, sandy country or dunes reaching

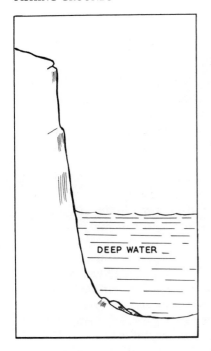

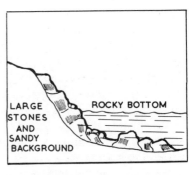

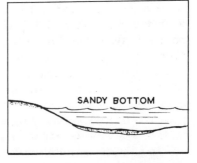

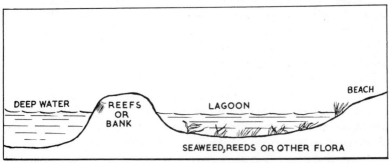

all the way down to the sea. You will find that very near the shore there will be sand banks, bars or other signs of shallow water further out.

If there is much vegetation all the way down to the very edge of the water you will find vegetation continuing below.

If the coast is made up of high cliffs going straight down it means that there will be deep water immediately off-shore, except in places where large boulders have rolled down from the mountain tops from time to time. In such a case, you will be swimming among these large boulders that have fallen into the sea.

On shores where the sand is coral sand and the general rock formation is dried coral rock, soft and easy to break off, it means that you are standing near coral reefs. The reef will either be a series of oases of coral in an underwater desert of sand and occasional shrubs, or you will find shallow water full of coral shrubbery, and small holes ending suddenly in a precipice over the edges off which the sea breaks.

In all of these places you will find fish. Let us have a closer look.

1. Rocks under water and shallow places further out. This is great fishing ground for the beginner. You may well find a rocky plateau about three to six metres under the water rising up from the sea bottom and surrounded by water going in depth down to, let us say, sixteen to twenty metres. It is as though there was just too much water for it to become an island. This is often the kind of place where groupers and other rock-dwelling fish have established their homes. It is the sort of place where passing fish stop for food and refuge. Fish of all kinds gather round these rocks at different times of the day and go about their business. At certain times of the day such places have all the characteristics of a water hole on the edge of an African jungle or plain, only fish, of course, gather to feed and not to drink. I have never been able to establish for sure the time of day or night when this happens. These are the places where bigger fish, coming in from the greater depths, find it profitable to make their raids for food. These submerged rocks, full of vegetation, are for bigger fish in some ways what chicken farms are for foxes. It is almost impossible to encounter bigger fish in shallow water except in places like this. If you are not yet ready to go for the bigger fish there are plenty of little ones busy grazing, or medium-sized fish passing in their search for pasture. You will soon begin to look upon the medium-sized fish as cattle or sheep, quietly grazing in a field. If you swim quietly among them, you will find that unless you make sudden movements the fish appear not to be frightened at all by your appearance, and will continue at their occupation. To them you seem to be a large Zeppelin quietly moving about their sky. You will be able to come quite near them and you may soon hope that you will be able to take a shot. You will then discover that though the fish seem to be quite unconcerned at your presence they are fully aware of the stranger in their midst. Most of them see far better than you do and their skins are very sensitive to vibrations. They are much quicker than you are. Their acute timidity is their greatest defence. If you make any kind of quick movement you will find they move from one place to another with lightning speed. Such cattle-like fish that go about in groups are, however, essentially rather more stupid than the lone rangers and you will find that they easily lose confidence. If you manage to transform yourself from a Zeppelin into a dive bomber and corner one of them, you will probably find that it will lose its head and try dashing about in one direction and another and very soon will pause, quite perplexed as to what to do next. Sometimes they are foolish enough to fly into a hole which has only one exit. This will be your moment. They will never run very far from you or their herd, so even if you have missed, taking a shot and reloading your gun will not cause all the fish to run away. You can therefore spend some time taking shots, reloading your gun and catching some fish without frightening the other fish too far away.

2. Coral reefs. These abound in fish food and are typical underwater scenery in the tropics. The smaller fish inhabit little holes in the shallow water and every hole or cave is worth inspecting. Along the edges of the reefs you will get places where rock-dwelling fish of various kinds have made their homes and the predatory fish from the deeper waters come in for food at various times of the day. The thing to do is to cruise quietly along the edge of the reef, always keeping half an eye on the sandy bottom nearby in case you come up against a jack or mackerel of some kind, or perhaps a barracuda. Mutton-fishes will also keep to the sand and make occasional forays into the coral jungle. Rays cruise along the edge and so do sharks. It will not take you long to realize that you must behave in your stalking much as a predatory fish would. If the edge of the coral reef is a steep cliff it will be worth while to make deep dives more or less 'on spec' from time to time because, if you look into a hole, you may suddenly come up against a grouper. Occasionally, if the coral reef is a forest of large corals, you will find that the scene under water is like a strange world of millions of underground passages teeming with fish, all of whom seem to

*Stalking. The spearfisherman is in the correct relaxed
position for a horizontal shot. He is wearing a full two-piece
wetsuit and cap and carries a torch in his left hand. There are
many good makes of pressurized torches.
Photograph by Roberto Dei*

know at least a hundred ways out of a difficult position through the maze of coral, while all you dare do is to poke about at the entrance of each hole or cave.

3. Large rocks near shore. The next best ground for the beginner is where you find large stones near the shore and large stones immediately under the surface. As you swim quietly over the rocks, around corners and promontories from the shore, you may suddenly encounter quite large fish. This is also the sort of region where you may come across groupers and other rock-dwelling fish. In Chapter 4, I shall discuss the technique of spearfishing in coral reefs and rocky shores.

4. Vegetation. If you choose to fish in waters where there is much vegetation, your greatest chance is to swim quietly along the surface and hope that you will surprise one of the fish quietly grazing among the submarine flora. Unless you are very quick you will probably find that the fish will disappear in the vegetation, and it is almost useless to remain where you are hoping that the fish will come up. This is, therefore, very chancy ground and especially in the waters of California and South Australia. It is not to be recommended for the beginner because he may very soon be disheartened.

5. Sandy bottom. The same applies to sandy bottoms where you will very rarely find fish. If you do, they have so much room to manœuvre here that they will simply swim away, and no man is quick enough, even with fins on his feet, to try to chase fish in the open sea. The only exceptions to this are fish of the sole family. These are difficult to see. They lie flat on the sand and take on almost perfectly all the local colours, usually covering themselves with a thin layer of sand. They move fairly slowly and if you are quick they are easy prey for you. The same applies to rays, stinging and otherwise. Please look up Chapter 7 for my criticisms of spearing rays and Chapter 8 for their characteristics and the method of stalking them, if you must.

6. Deep water. Next we look at fishing in water that is rather deep for the diver who does not use compressed-air or oxygen apparatus. Essentially it is very much the same as fishing along the rocky

shores. Your chances of finding fish are smaller in deep water because you have to take frequent deep dives, look around and come
up again for air. This is a very exhausting business. There are many
young men nowadays, especially in the Mediterranean, who have to
dive twenty metres each time. Here, however, is where, once you
have become an experienced diver, you can achieve the greatest
element of surprise with your sudden dive to the depths. You
may find quite large fish quietly cruising near the rocks on the sea
bed, never expecting you to come along.

Where the coast is very steep and rocky you may find underwater caves. If you approach the mouth of a cave very carefully
you may suddenly encounter fish that use the cave as a home or
temporary refuge. The best thing to do if you have plenty of time
is to lie hidden from view and wait for fish coming in or going out.
When you have become more experienced you may venture to
dive down and enter caves, but the thing to remember in such a
case is to be very careful that the entrance to the cave is big enough
for you to turn around and come up for air again without hitting
the rocks with your head or any other part of your body. You
should avoid going so deep into a cave that you cannot make a
quick and efficient return. Before entering a cave you should make
sure that you can reach the surface outside it or that there is
sufficient headroom of air inside the cave to enable you to come to
the surface without leaving the cave after each dive. No beginner
should attempt to enter a cave unless the sea is like a millpond and
there is no swell.

Along many steep coasts it is often fun swimming close to the
rocky wall which sometimes drops straight down to impenetrable
depths. On closer observation, with frequent diving to inspect
almost every hole, you will find fish previously hidden from your
view. Often you will come upon the ugly head of a moray peering
at you in apparent agony, as though it were breathing its last.

7. Port fishing. If you can bear bathing in smelly waters, which
I cannot, you will find good fishing at entrances to most ports.
Fish follow ships and sailing boats into port, feeding on what is
thrown overboard. The same conditions prevail inside the break-
waters too, but you must at all times be very careful of craft overhead, anglers along the shore and people dropping anchors or
discharging oil or rubbish.

'Bermuda, here we come, eh, Mr. Stanton?'

3

EQUIPMENT AND TRAINING

The most sportful fishes dare not jest with the edge-tools of this Dead Sea. THOMAS FULLER
A Pisgah-Sight of Palestine, ii, xiii, 1650 A.D.

Difficile est tenere, quae accepteris, nisi exerceas.
(It is difficult to retain the knowledge you have acquired unless you put it into practice.) PLINY
Letters, Bk viii, epis. 14, c. 108 A.D.

THE GOGGLE

It has never been established who invented the goggle; as I have said already, I have heard from Renzo Avanzo of two Japanese visiting Naples and diving there in 1911, but I have not been able to confirm this. All I have been able to find out in over thirty-six years of intense interest in the world under the sea is that the goggle was first made by the Japanese, or possibly someone else in the Eastern Pacific.

In 1952 I went diving in Ago Bay, Japan, with the girls who worked in Mr Mikimoto's pearl grounds. They used the simplest type of goggle—two small glass plates, one over each eye—and I tried to find out who had invented them and when. But I could not make them understand and all I got was giggles! They dived without fins and rolled about with uncontrollable laughter when I, with my fins, beat them to the bottom and back.

On the same trip I came across Japanese net fishermen. Some of these went into the water at the last minute, as the nets were gradually being closed near the shore, to supervise the operation and chase straying fish into the nets. They also wore goggles, but these were made of wood and tied around their heads with string or cotton strips. Here too the historian in me was frustrated.

There is little doubt, however, that goggles (similar to those worn by early motorists against wind and dust, and those that racing drivers and motor cycle riders still wear today) were the first thing used by swimmers and divers who did not go in for diving with a helmet. We might as well go on calling these two glass windows tied to the head in a wood or rubber frame by their original name of goggle.

The view of underwater life when wearing goggles is exactly the same as seeing fish in an aquarium, so even if you never succeed in catching a fish you will have had an experience you will never forget.

It was found, however, that these first goggles suffered from two great disadvantages. The first was that the two lenses pressed on the eyes and nose and caused pain especially if the swimmer had a Greek profile. The reason for this is that the air inside the goggle fitted on the shore remains at sea-level pressure. As you descend below the surface the pressure of water on the outside of the goggle increases while the pressure of the air inside the goggle remains the same. The goggle is thus forced to press more and more against your eyes, causing severe pain. Moreover, nobody can fit the goggle in exactly the same position over both eyes. Increasing pressure will cause different pressure on each eye, causing double vision. The other disadvantage is that with a goggle the nose is free. The deeper you go the more water, at heavy pressure, will enter your nose and even press on the sinus entrances, causing water bubbles to collect inside your ear/nose/throat system, and severe pain.

An improvement on these goggles was the type which had one kidney-shaped window which fitted over your eyes, leaving the nose outside. This eliminated double vision. Both these goggles are only satisfactory when used on the surface; for instance, they are useful for protecting the eyes from disinfectants in swimming pools. A further development was a pair of rubber balls attached to the goggles on each side of the face. These balls were connected with the inside of the goggle through a small orifice. As the diver descended, the air in the balls passed into the goggle so that the pressure on the inside of the goggle became equal to the pressure

Goggles and masks

Above: *Original type of goggle where the nose is exposed. For any depth except just below the surface, a nose clip must be used. The kidney-shaped mask has put both eyes behind one glass plate to prevent double vision and the balls contain extra air to relieve pressure of mask on the face at depth. Nose clip must be used.*

Centre: *Large full-face mask for use by surface swimmers. Smallest type of mask which incorporates rubber nose cover thus enabling diver to snort into the mask to equalize the pressure in the nose and inner ear spaces with water pressure outside.*

Below: *Original Pinnochio mask by Cressi of Italy, the precursor of all masks allowing pressure equalization by nose pinching. This is now also possible on almost all one plate oval masks, as shown.*

of water on the outside. Sometimes an even larger quantity of air was stored in a rubber bag at the back of the head.

THE MASK

A further improvement has produced a contraption consisting simply of one fairly large oval window. Here the nose was inside and the pair of goggles thus became one mask. By snorting air through the nose into this mask when under the water, a diver can equalize the pressure inside it to the pressure of the water on the mask at the depth at which he may find himself. This is the mask most widely used all over the world.

Finally, Cressi of Italy came up with a great improvement. Instead of having the nose and eyes covered by a single oval plate, he produced a kidney-shaped plate with the rubber part extended to cover the nose. The great advantage here was that as you dived deeper, you could pinch the tip of your nose through the rubber with thumb and forefinger. The extra air pressure created by blowing through your nose and pressing air against the pinching thumb and forefinger was enough to clear a passage of free air inside your lung/mouth/nose/throat/Eustachian tube/middle ear system to include the air in the mask. This equalized the pressure inside your inner air system and inside the mask to the pressure of the water on the outside of the mask and also to the pressure of the water on the outside of the eardrums. Once the flow of air was free, the system adjusted itself to all the different pressures from the water outside—but more of this in Chapters 5 and 6.

Cressi called his mask 'The Pinocchio' after the famous Italian fictional wooden boy whose nose grew if he lied. Cressi's imitators have been legion. They all provide some way of squeezing the tip of your nose with thumb and forefinger for pressure equalizing purposes.

Ross Doe in Bermuda and José Beltrán of Majorca were pioneers in the early fifties of the smallest possible mask consistent with the widest possible angle of unhampered vision. The end of the 1953 season in Italy, the land of the pioneer of the Pinocchio mask, saw this tendency growing. The argument used to explain this drift to the smallest possible mask is that the bigger and heavier masks contained too much air and were thus too buoyant, and it is true that any loss of excess buoyancy makes for easier diving. The development of masks with a non-return valve at the tip of the nose, which in theory helped you to let the last drops of water inside the mask seep out, was unsuccessful as the non-return valve has so far proved to be inefficient.

You may find that a mist forms on the inside of your mask. This is especially true of the full face mask with two built-in breathing tubes. In addition to the heat from your face on the inner surface of the glass, there is also the hot air expelled through the nose. One way of preventing this mist forming is to wash the inside of your mask very thoroughly in water before use. Keep water in it until the last moment before use so that both the inside and the outside are the same temperature as the water. Before putting your mask on, splash water on your face too. You will know that you have removed any greasy spots still on the glass or that you have removed thin layers of yesterday's sea salt crystals if you dip the mask in the water and then take it out again. If the mask is clean it is ready for use. The glass will then remain uniformly wet and clear on both sides. If the water runs away from some spots, rub those spots with sea water until they disappear. There are dozens of aids you can use to hurry this process of making your mask mistproof. Spitting and rubbing was thought of first, then came raw potatoes and onions, then tobacco and seaweed and the chemicals used to clean ordinary spectacles. I have also found all detergents very useful. Avoid lifting your mask on to your forehead or hair as this is one way of getting grease on the glass. Only those who do not use their masks seriously adopt this attitude.

Early models had a simple rubber strap which usually slipped when wet or greasy. There is always some grease about one's fingers. Nowadays the rubber straps have ribs or blisters to prevent slipping and Cressi has pioneered a strap-locking device. The difference this tiny improvement has made to a diver's comfort is enormous. I cannot stress too strongly the all-important point of having the mask fitting tightly and comfortably. Not until this is achieved can one possibly enjoy the necessary relaxation and freedom of movement upon which everything else in this book depends. Masks should be thoroughly washed in fresh water after use and when not in use they, together with the snorkels and straps, should be kept covered with talcum powder.

Short-sighted people can now have their prescription lens ground into the tempered glass of the mask.

THE SNORKEL

The trouble with all types of goggle or mask is that they leave you with the problem of surface breathing still unsolved. The invention of the breathing tube or 'snorkel' meant that a swimmer could have his face and most of his body just below the surface and still breathe through the tube which remained out of the water. It has been found in practice that these breathing tubes should not be more than about thirty centimetres long. The only problem to be faced is that even fairly small waves may cause water to come down the tube and flood your mask. You will soon learn to hold your head in such a position that, when you are swimming along the surface, the waves do not cover your snorkel. Originally, these snorkels were equipped with a lever contraption at the top with a cork affixed to it. This served as a valve so that when you dived below the water the tube was automatically closed by the other end of the lever. The moment you came up above the surface and the top of your snorkel tube was in the air, the weight of the cork would reopen the valve and you would be able to breathe again. Some masks had two breathing tubes built in and the others had a small aluminium barrel or table tennis ball instead of the cork. However, these all proved unsatisfactory as they were unable to prevent water from entering the snorkel as the swimmer dived deeper, so they have been discarded.

If you use any of the goggles or masks I have described you should have a separate snorkel. Otherwise, when swimming along the surface you will have to pause for breath from time to time. This means turning your head in order to get your nose or mouth out of the water. You thus take your eyes off the scene under the water, and it is extremely difficult and tiring to stalk fish in this fashion. It means that your picture of the situation below will be like a series of short scenes in a film instead of one uninterrupted sequence.

The snorkel consists of a metal or plastic tube, as illustrated. The rubber mouthpiece is put firmly into the mouth, two small hard bits of rubber being provided to enable you to grip the mouthpiece with your teeth. These snorkels are usually provided with a rubber or plastic band in the form of a pince-nez, which is attached to the rubber band holding the mask to your face (see illustration). If you use a snorkel you must be quite sure that you

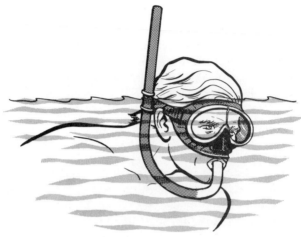

Snorkels
Swimming on the surface with a modern snorkel.

Top and centre: *Simple snorkel showing two positions of telescopic length adjusting.*
Below: *Simplest possible snorkel is the best. Two plastic connected rings allow mask head band to slide through loosely attaching snorkel to mask.*

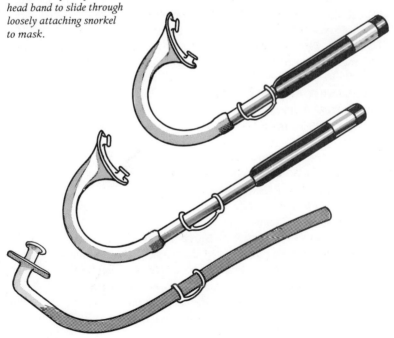

do not breathe once you are below the surface, otherwise you will breathe in water. When you come up to the surface again you must resist your natural inclination to breathe in some fresh air. You must first of all use the air that has remained in your lungs to blow out the water which has entered the tube. As you descend, the water, at increasing pressure, squeezes the air in the tube. As snorkels are no longer fitted with corks or table tennis balls, you will have to learn to blow out any water that may have entered your mouth, once you reach the surface.

You will find that when you put on your mask and put your snorkel into your mouth you will feel extremely clumsy, and the odds are that you will think you will never overcome all the difficulties in your way. The first thing to remember is that you must only breathe through your mouth. This is a rather difficult job for those of us who have never learned to swim using the mouth for breathing.

For those who only wish to swim on the surface, there is a full-face mask covering eyes, nose and mouth (the type with two snorkels built-in, as illustrated).

As a matter of fact, two of the greatest spearfishermen I have known used masks covering eyes and nose, without using any kind of snorkel. They simply turned their heads and took in air with their mouths opened as wide as possible and then held their breath for as long as possible. I tried to do this and found it very tiring to take a breath every forty seconds or so and then take deep dives in between, but I have spent days with Rodney Jonklaas in Ceylon and Jack Ackerman among the Hawaiian Islands and they managed very well.

THE FINS

Equipped with a mask and snorkel you are in fact quite ready to do what the Americans call 'snorkeling'. By using your one free hand and your legs you can move about quite freely along the surface of the water and you can dive below the surface in order to approach your quarry. Even if you are an excellent swimmer, however, you will find that you are far too slow for most fish. It will take you some time to reach a depth of three or four metres. The effort of doing so will tire you and you will be able to stay very little time at that depth.

Rubber fins were first developed in about 1939 or 1940, probably by Owen Churchill of California. They are attached to the feet and give the swimmer, using the crawl stroke with the legs, a tremendous increase in surface speed. You will even be able to swim at quite a respectable speed by using your legs only. If, when you are

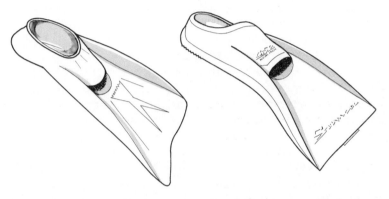

Cressi revolutionized fins with his floating Rondine (left) with protected heel and space for toes to move, thus avoiding cramp. There are now many similar makes, of which one is illustrated.

lying horizontally along the surface, you take a deep breath and double up your body as though making a deep bow so that your head points almost vertically downwards under the water and you use your free hand, you can get yourself to a depth of about two metres under water in the space of a second. If you continue poised vertically downwards with your head and then begin using your feet in the crawl stroke, you will find that with fins you will shoot downwards at a speed you hardly thought was possible. Within a second or two you will find yourself at a depth of about five or six metres. By changing the position of your body under the water at that depth so that your head points upwards, and by keeping your body quite straight, and again using the crawl stroke with your legs, you will find that you will shoot up towards the surface just as quickly as you came down. I myself have never in my life been able to go below a depth of about ten metres without the use of the fins but with them I find (even at sixty years of age) that I can reach a depth of eighteen to twenty metres, stay down below for a few seconds, and come up again. This is nothing sensational, and almost any decent swimmer can achieve it with a little practice. Most readers will probably be familiar with the exploits of 'frogmen' during the last war. These men were able to cover enormous distances under water, lay mines or remove them and generally explore the situation below the surface. Equipped with oxygen or compressed air-breathing apparatus and fins, they were able to cover great distances without coming up for air. They could never have achieved all this without fins. You must get a pair of fins that fit your feet exactly. There are several types on the market, and with most of them you will be able to achieve the results I have described above. I find that flexibility and width at both sides of the foot are more useful than length. I have only illustrated two versions of one type of fins. These, originally invented by Cressi of Italy, cover the heel and have a hole to allow the toes to move. Fins should have these holes through which the toes almost protrude. This gives the whole foot the facility to move a little inside the fin and avoids cramp in the calves. Fins vary in the quality of the rubber. Most of them can now float, which is an advantage if they are dropped overboard. There are fins with adjustable straps for use on varying sizes of feet. They come in many colours. I myself do not allow black ones on my boat as they leave marks on my white non-slip plastic on deck. They should be washed in fresh water, dried after use and always kept out of the sun.

They have all sorts of names: 'Swim-fins', 'Duck-feet', 'Flippers', 'Web-feet', 'Frog-feet', but 'Fins' has by now found almost universal acceptance, where English is spoken.

SPEARS

Your weapon is the spear. All the models you will find for sale in the shops are developments of the simple land spear. The essential problem which underwater fishermen have had to face was to substitute some method of powerful projection of the spear for the simple force of the human arm.

When spearfishing began in Europe most amateurs forged their own weapons. I made my first spear in 1937 from the ribs of my father's umbrella. There have been countless variations of the same weapon, but there are only two or three main types in use today.

The first is where the method of propelling the spear is the same as with an ordinary sling or catapult. The spear is propelled towards the fish by the action of stretching a piece of rubber, which holds the blunt end of the spear, and then releasing it. The other two main methods in use today are the release of the spear by means of a metal spring or release by means of compressed air. In the first method the spear is pressed down the barrel of a gun, inside which there is a spring which is thus compressed or stretched, depending on the type used, and shooting consists of simply releasing the spring which then sends the spear on its way towards the fish. In the second method there are all sorts of models working on the principle of the explosive release of compressed air or, sometimes, carbon dioxide from little cylinders.

To save confusion, I shall assume that the reader is righthanded and that he or she prefers to use the right eye for aiming.

1. **The Hawaiian or Polynesian Sling.** This is the simplest and cheapest of all and is the first development of the most primitive instrument. It usually consists of an aluminium, plastic, or wooden tube which is held in the left hand. A strong elastic rubber band is fixed at one end of this tube so that, when one inserts the spear through the other end, one can stretch the rubber with the right hand gripping the tube with the left hand. The blunt end of the spear is held by the thumb and the first two fingers of the right hand, together with the rubber band, like a sling. The rubber band is stretched as far as possible. The tube is held as near as possible to the right eye in order to achieve the best aim. The spear is then suddenly released by letting go with the right hand. The spears in this case are usually very light in weight since your arm cannot stretch a long elastic rubber band sufficiently far to gain reasonable momentum with a heavier spear. These spears are not connected with the holding tube by a line, so that when you have released your spear and missed you have to dive down again to retrieve it. If you have speared a fish you must also dive down again to get it. This weapon should thus not be used by the beginner at depths over three metres as it involves frequent diving to the depths. Safety catches are fitted to some models but they should not be relied on.

Jack Ackerman of Hawaii, perhaps the most celebrated spearfisherman of the Pacific, is the great proponent of the Hawaiian sling. He, however, does not use two hands for shooting. He holds his wood or aluminium tube in his right hand. He inserts his two-

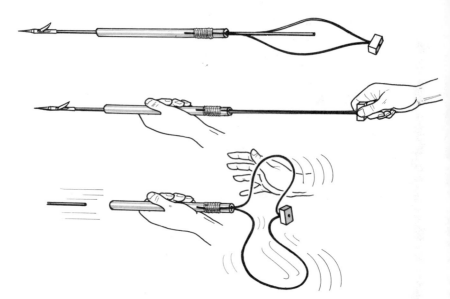

Two ways of using Hawaiian sling.

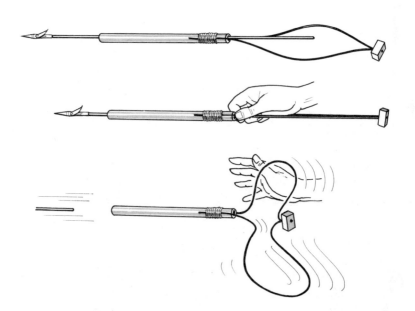

metre aluminium spear with his left hand, stretching the rubber as far as it will go. Then he presses his right thumb hard on the spear at the rear end of the tube keeping the stretched rubber (as in my illustration) in place and preventing it from shooting out, more or less the way you would hold a hose to prevent water pouring out. He then dives, using his left hand for swimming. He does not have to pause at the sea bed to cock his spear, an operation that takes time and involves movements which will frighten most fish. The operation of cocking the spear at depths using both hands inevitably tends to bring the diver towards the surface. Ackerman avoids all this. He is always ready to shoot. Moreover, he can gain distance under a rock by holding the rock with his left hand and putting his right arm deep inside the rock as far as it will go, and then releasing the spear by lifting his right thumb. I find this method of spearfishing most attractive. It is the most difficult and therefore most sporting. My right thumb ached so violently when I first tried it that I could only fire four or five shots at a time before pausing to regain my strength. I have seen Jack Ackerman fish all morning and I suppose his right thumb must by now be one of the strongest on earth.

The only sure way of landing big fish inside a rock with this light spear is to hit the fish in the brain, killing it instantly. Jack Ackerman holds the world's record for pompano (or pampano) with a catch of fifty-eight kilogrammes (127 pounds) which he killed with a light spear used in the manner described above. The pompano ('Ulua' in Hawaiian) belongs to the Family *Carangidae* which in English are variously described as kingfishes, jacks or queenfishes. If the fish is hit in the middle of its body, Ackerman continues his dive. Upon reaching the wounded fish he pushes the spear through the body and holds the spear with both hands, one on each side of the fish.

2. Other Sling Models. These are all developments of the original sling or catapult model which is, of course, the lightest in weight.

(a) A long time ago Dr Hans Hass constructed a light wood pole three centimetres in diameter and about two metres long, with a strong thin metal point. Having soon discovered that the power of this spear thrust forward under water by his arm was not great enough to provide it any penetration power, let alone speed, he

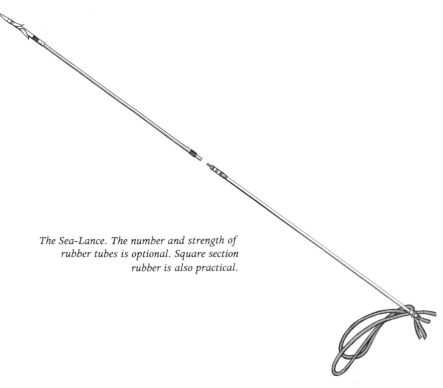

*The Sea-Lance. The number and strength of
rubber tubes is optional. Square section
rubber is also practical.*

provided his pole with a strong rubber sling fixed at the blunt end
by a strong cord. This sling is gripped by the right hand between
thumb and forefinger and is then stretched as far as it will go.
Then, with the sling still held stretched to its utmost between
thumb and forefinger, the pole is gripped tightly by the whole
hand at a place as near the spear point as the stretched sling will
allow. To hit a fish one must have the point within thirty centimetres of the target, and all that needs to be done is to release the
pole suddenly. It will shoot out at great speed for about thirty
centimetres and the sling will remain loose between the thumb and
forefinger. This pole can be ready for the next shot in less than a
second, unlike all other models. I always use a development of this
model of Dr Hass's, made of fibreglass in America but also of
aluminium in America and Australia. It is about two metres long
and in some cases can be unscrewed into two or three parts that are
easily carried in a golf bag. I have been able to dive with this spear,

shoot it at a fish, miss and load it again, all still using the same breath, an operation that is quite impossible with any other weapon. In America its trade name is the Sea Lance.

(b) The simplest form of the European models consists of a non-rusting metal barrel about one metre long along which the spear is inserted into a catch mechanism on the outside of the barrel. The rubber band has been replaced by a solid piece of elastic rubber pipe fixed to the tip of the barrel and this is divided into two parts by a small V-shaped wire joint. The base of the spear has a groove into which this V-shaped joint can be fixed by stretching the rubber pipe. The spear is released by pulling a trigger provided on a handle resembling an ordinary pistol or revolver handle. Some models have been strengthened by the use of three, four or even more rubber pipes in the same manner. All parts of the gun itself, as well as the spear, are made of non-rusting metal. The disadvantage of these models is in the fact that the rubber pipes sooner or later begin to rot as a result of contact with salt water. However, these rubber pipes are easily replaced and do not cost a great deal. Even

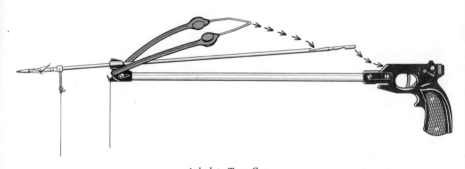

Arbalete Type Gun

before salt water has had its rotting effect the rubber is apt to become overstretched as a result of constant use. The great advantage of these more highly developed models, the best of them of French manufacture and called Arbaletes, is that they are held cocked to a degree which the human arm could not long hold in check. These guns are easy to handle; they do not weigh very much and can be held in one hand for long periods of time so that the other hand is free for swimming. There are many versions of the rubber sling guns, all justly celebrated for their great penetration power at close range. The rubber sling guns usually have the holding handle at the back of the gun and thus two hands are needed to steady it and fire it. In some models this disadvantage has been somewhat alleviated by the addition of another handle in the middle. Another disadvantage of these models is that the rubber charging system and the small total weight makes for greater resistance to side movements in water and consequent loss of aiming speed. Sometimes, and especially when the rubber is new, it requires great strength to load these guns. The rubber pipe is stretched with both hands pulling the V-shaped joint towards the blunt end of the spear with the back of the gun against one's belly or knee.

3. **Metal Spring Guns.** There are many models of this gun and in France, Italy and Spain it was the type used most frequently until about ten years ago. The power of this gun depended on the length and strength of the spring which was used in the barrel. In most models the spear was pressed down the muzzle of the barrel until a click indicated that the gun was cocked. The spear was released by pressing the trigger fitted to the handle in much the same way as on the sling type guns. These models are usually heavier, and therefore more difficult and tiring to handle. The longer and more powerful the spring is, the longer the barrel must be. Therefore the force to compress the spring when inserting the spear down the muzzle must also be stronger. This makes loading the gun in water a more difficult and more tiring job. In time, and if the spring is not cleaned with fresh water after every use and greased with water-resisting grease, it may lose some of its strength. However, in many years of use with intervals of many months in storage in between, none of my Italian, Spanish or French springs have lost any appreciable strength. Most spring guns have holes

bored all along the barrel to permit water to be ejected as the spring is released. It is easy to use two of these holes equidistant from the end to fix the support-pin for the slackened spring so that it may be compressed into a shorter space, thus regaining some of its lost force.

Much has been written of the comparative force of rubber and spring guns. Tests carried out by Jack Prodanovich and Don Clark in the air in California favoured the rubber-propelled French Arbalete, but a searching test made by Gustav DallaValle, the famous Italian spearfisherman who used to live in Haiti, favoured Cressi's Italian spring guns, which confirms Rodney Jonklaas's long and spectacular experiences in the waters of Ceylon. One should remember that a proper test for a gun is its penetration power at short range under water. Most good guns, whether rubber or spring, should be quite satisfactory to the sporting spearfisherman, who does not dive under the sea with the intention of committing wholesale murder. The disadvantage of the really strong spring guns is that they are very long and thus clumsy to use among closely placed rocks. All long guns can now be dismantled for easier packing and carrying, and a golf bag is an ideal carrier.

4. The Simple Spear. In the early fifties, Henry Tiarks developed a four-metre simple spear one centimetre thick, of very strong stainless steel. The spear gun can be dismantled into two or three parts for travelling purposes. Tiarks and Ross Doe, the famous Bermuda spearfisherman, have been very successful with these simple spears in spite of the fact that these weapons were not fitted with barbs. I have watched Ross Doe using one of these in Bermuda. He swims along the surface, balancing the long thin spear between his neck and his shoulder, using both arms for swimming. The thinness of the spear prevents the larger fish from noticing the approach of the point. Holding the spear nearer the blunt end, Ross Doe drives it into his quarry with a sudden lunge of his arm, so that about two metres of the spear protrudes on each side of the fish. The speared fish is then left to itself for a few seconds while Ross Doe comes up for air. Another dive enables him to go down, grip the spear on each side of the fish, and bring it up. The fish is not able to wriggle off such a long spear in the short time available to it before the second dive, even though there are no barbs on the spear.

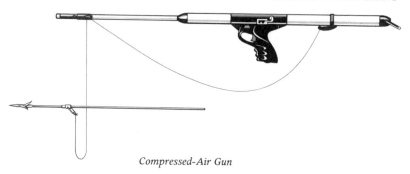

Compressed-Air Gun

5. The Compressed-Air Gun. Spaniards pioneered this type of gun which has a compressed-air chamber. The top of the barrel is strengthened and so constructed as to prevent the strong metal piston from flying out or the air from escaping. The spear is inserted down the muzzle and it fits lightly into the piston. The spear and piston are rammed down the barrel until a click indicates that the piston is beyond the catch connected with the trigger. About two hundred strokes with a bicycle pump or an equivalent dash of air from a motor tyre air compressor will provide enough propulsive force to make the gun superior to the best spring guns. The loss of air is very small, and one charging has lasted me a full month of daily use. In other respects the gun resembles the long spring guns. There are now many beautifully machined Italian compressed-air guns in addition to the original and much improved Spanish gun.

6. The Carbon-Dioxide Gun. There are several versions of this cartridge-loaded or cylinder weapon, mainly of American and Australian make. Although they vary somewhat, I find that they are all very powerful and very handy. They are, in fact, so good (and thus hardly sporting except for big game such as sharks) that I hesitate to mention them in a book for beginners. They are now banned almost everywhere.

With the exception of the Hawaiian sling, the Hass pole or Sea Lance and the Tiarks-Doe spear, all guns are provided with a line attaching the spear to the gun by means of a solid metal, plastic or spring runner, which can slide up and down the spear, so constructed that it will not slip off at either end. This prevents unnecessary diving for the harpoon after missing a fish and it also enables the fisherman to hold on to the speared fish. The length of the line used to be such that a fisherman could breathe on the surface and still be able to hold on to a gun with the point of the spear in the fish or stuck into a rock ten metres below to prevent it being lost. The exact length of the line thus depended on the length of the fisherman's arm, the length of the gun and the spear.

Three of the many types of sliding runners which keep the spear attached to the gun.

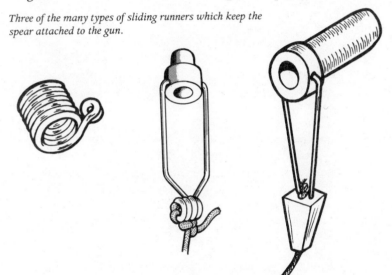

Such a long line, let loose to float freely in the water, will wind itself round one's feet in no time in choppy water. It shows the cunning of a living being in the way it will find places where it will get hooked up just as one is about to dive or shoot. Spearfishermen then fitted reels to their guns. I have found braided nylon cord to be the best for the line. It will not curl, it will not rot and, provided it is thick enough, it will hold almost anything. I use 100 or 200 kilogramme (three hundred- or four hundred-pound) test braided nylon cord and twelve metres will just go on a ten-centimetre reel. I have also a line of 500 kilogramme test nylon cord but this will, of course, not go on any reel of a size that is practical under water. It has to be attached lightly along the whole length of the barrel and wound back and forth say four times along

Speared Mediterranean Sea Bass. Note the short Italian compressed-air gun and the almost perfect penetration point of the spear.
Photograph by Roberto Dei

a two-metre gun. This method of attachment can also be used with a thinner line if a reel is found clumsy.

Great strength may be thought excessive even for larger fish, but I once lost a stingray in Bali no more than twenty kilogrammes in weight using a 100-kilogramme test cord. The moment the ray managed to pull at my line round a coral rock it managed to break it. This has also happened to me with sharks.

In the last few years the Italians have realized that a long line was more of a nuisance than it was worth. So the line is now no longer than two metres and no reel is used. If the fish has been hit or the spear is embedded in a rock, repeated dives will retrieve it.

For fishing really big fish, such as sharks, I have used a very strong line attached to an inflatable rubber cushion (with CO_2 gas released from a little cylinder as on an airplane lifebelt) carried folded in my left hand. This is a cumbersome type of equipment not at all suitable for beginners.

Rodney Jonklaas, who is assistant Superintendent of the Colombo Zoological Gardens and one of the world's most expert spearfishermen, uses a steel line ten metres long fixed, back and forth, along the barrel of his gun. He is a man of infinite patience and consummate skill. I was constantly cutting myself when I used a steel line, but I have seen him fish for hours without ever losing his temper.

Most gunmakers claim a range for their weapons far in excess of their actual performance, so far as I have been able to judge. Claims vary between a range—an effective underwater range—of three metres to six metres. I have tested many guns and it is indeed true that spears will, in most cases, when shot horizontally under water at a depth no greater than sixty centimetres, go these distances. However, the speed of the spear is so slow in the last part of its trajectory that by the time it reaches its target the target is there no more. In practice you should try to approach your fish so that the point of your spear is at most not more than a metre or two away from your target. If you have a powerful gun your chances of spearing your fish are increased considerably, but even with the weakest gun you have an excellent chance of spearing your fish from a distance from the top of the spear of one metre. This chance increases, of course, if you are above the fish and the direction of your spear when released is nearer the downward vertical.

Exposing the metal parts of your gun to salt water causes them to rust very quickly. It is therefore advisable to wash your gun in fresh water every time you have used it, even if it is claimed to be made of non-rusting metal, and then to grease the spring if it is a spring gun. I have used whale grease and water-resistant grease, but I have also found ordinary grease used for motor-cars to be just as effective. Care should be taken to remove all grains of sand adhering to your gun as soon after use as you can. The metal spring itself should be thickly coated with grease all the time. Rubber sling and compressed-air guns are less trouble to maintain.

SPEAR POINTS

The spear used with a Hawaiian sling is simply a thin aluminium rod coming to a point. Since the penetration power of the spear is not great, a barb in the form of a movable wing is attached very near the point itself. There is no need to have a detachable head on this spear. A fish, if speared, can be slipped off the other end. You will find that these spears bend very easily, especially when bigger fish are speared, but if you place a bent spear on a hard horizontal surface you can hammer it back into its original shape in a matter of minutes. A decent hammer is so much more useful for this purpose than more elaborate tools that I advise you to carry one with you.

I have already mentioned that the Tiarks-Doe long spear carries no barb at all, the fisherman relying on the length of the spear to prevent the fish from wriggling off.

Novice spearfishermen using rubber, spring-powered or compressed-air guns will very quickly find that a good number of their shots miss the fish and their spears hit rocks. This can seldom be avoided even when the novice has become a practised shot. Most fish worth shooting at are in or near rocks. The development of all guns, rubber or spring-propelled or compressed-air, has gone in the direction of giving high penetration power at short range. Only luck will enable you to spear a fish more than two metres away from the spear point at the time of firing. Either the fish will no longer be at the spot where you aimed your shot, or water resistance together with the resistance produced by your line will decrease the speed at which the spear travels to such an extent that it will, at best, just touch or graze your quarry two metres away.

The spearfisherman will thus be rather rough with his spear.

Most spears nowadays are made of hard steel or a strong alloy of steel and aluminium, which will stand repeated hits at rocks from a few feet away.

Even so, spears now have detachable spear points which can be screwed on and off easily. It is well for the beginner to have a good supply of these spare points. He will thus save himself much expense by reducing his supply of spare spears.

I have illustrated a number of spear points. The old-fashioned trident (which I have not shown) should be mentioned first. Its obvious advantage lies in the fact that it has three points and the chance of hitting a fish is thus increased. But the trident will lose speed more quickly than other points and taking a fish off its fixed barbs is a messy business. The beginner should abandon it as soon as he can. It gets less sporting and more messy as proficiency

More complicated spear points
Left: *Point with replaceable tip. The two wires can be fixed over the wire barbs so that the fish can be slid off without unscrewing spear point.* Centre: *Detachable head held to spear point by steel wire. The whole head should get buried in the fish. The wire will allow the fish to struggle freely and the spear is therefore not damaged and easier to hold than if a big fish were exercising its force on the spear itself. Rubber band or wooden wedge will keep detachable tip in place till moment of impact.* Right: *Elaborate point which incorporates barb-holder for sliding fish off and loading lever which obviates carrying separate loader.*

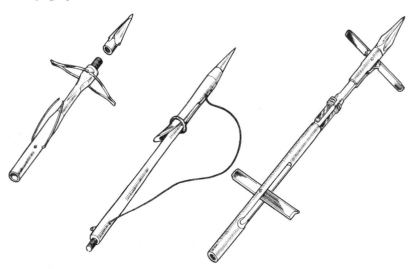

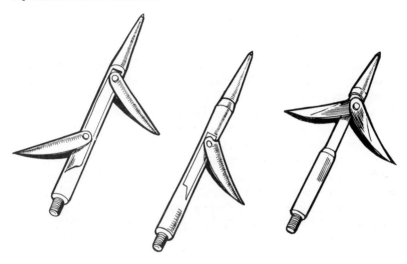

Most common and practical spear points
They often come with a tip that can be unscrewed and replaced.

increases. I have seen such heads with four or even five points but will not even look up the correct names for these developments of the trident. Let Neptune keep these himself to pose with for his fancier portraits. Humans should avoid them if they have any regard for honour or 'face'.

The next development was a movable wing barb on a single strong steel point. This consists of one or two wings fitted near the tip. These wings cannot move higher up towards the tip than at right angles to the spear itself. They may be U-shaped in section so that when pressed down the spear they are flush or almost flush with it, or they may fit into the body of the spear point to achieve the best streamlining possible. A well-aimed shot at a fish from a fairly short distance will pierce it beyond at least the first of these movable wings.

There are many variations of these wings, some being more efficient than others, and the illustrations show several types. They should be loose enough to achieve streamlining when the spear is in flight or piercing the fish. If they are too loose, however, the joint attaching them to the spear point may not be strong enough and the wing will come off if a big fish tugs hard.

I have also illustrated two types of spear points in which the wings can be pressed down parallel and flush with the spear point and held in that position either by two pins or a metal or rubber ring. These types are useful because the fish, (once it has been speared and the wings held down by the pins or rings), can be slipped off the spear without unscrewing the spear point. In a later chapter I shall elaborate on the matter of 'landing' your catch. For the time being I would merely like the reader to remember that there are some spear points that enable him to take the fish off the spear without unscrewing the spear point itself.

There is a further variation of the spear point in which the last two centimetres or so of the very tip can be unscrewed and changed.

Some fishermen use a spear point with a removable wing. This is attached loosely on top of the spear point and held lightly in a streamlined position by a rubber ring or matchstick. It is held fast to the spear point by a strand of fifteen-centimetre (six-inch) long wire. When the spear point enters the body of a large fish, the wing itself stays inside the fish, thus forming a larger and stronger barb than is otherwise possible without making the spear too clumsy. There are several other forms of this partly-detachable spear point.

Jack Prodanovich, the President of the Bottom Scratchers Club of San Diego, the most venerated spearfishing club in America, has a development of the first such elaborate partly-detachable spear point. This movable wing is attached to a Mae West* tied to his body in such a way that with one and the same tug the self-inflating mechanism is set to work and the Mae West is detached from his body. It would take a big fish indeed to take the Mae West down to the depths with it, if the fish has been speared on the surface. I used one of these once on a shark at a depth of thirty metres and, due to the pressure of the surrounding water, the Mae West only inflated to a third of its volume. I lost spear, line, Mae West—and shark.

Prodanovich, incidentally, was also one of the first who developed a powerhead for his spears. The charge explodes on impact, but the spear point remains attached to the spear. Prodanovich told me in 1952 that he only used his power head on big groupers or jewfish or sharks weighing not less than a hundred kilogrammes (two hun-

*For the benefit of younger readers, a Mae West is an airman's life jacket.

dred pounds). In America, one of these is produced commercially, under the name 'Thunderhead', which is claimed to be safe. Relief valves prevent backfires even when solid rock is hit and a safety-catch mechanism permits its use as an ordinary spear head. This is certainly a useful weapon for those spearfishermen intent on being photographed with monsters of the deep. A big grouper of a hundred kilogrammes or so will not be frightened of a man coming very close to him. A shot at his brain from about thirty centimetres away will kill him instantly. Only relatively little effort, none of it connected in any way with sport, will bring the dead fish to the surface and into a triumphant photograph.

Prodanovich, however, is more valiant than that. He has attacked sharks large enough to absorb the impact of the explosion and the spear point itself without turning a hair—if they had one. The big sharks just swam quietly away. He has paid for his pioneering experiments with the power head by losing his eye in an accident while firing a rubber-propelled spear with a power head in a swimming pool. I have been spearfishing with him since, and he has managed to adjust his shooting technique so well that he is just as successful now shooting righthanded and using his left eye. Beginners should avoid powerheads.

LOADERS

The loading of the gun by pressing the spear down the muzzle of the barrel presents considerable difficulties under water when spring or compressed-air guns are used. Loading, which I will describe more fully later, requires great strength to push the spear down the barrel and it is almost impossible to do this with the bare hand. As likely as not, the spring will suddenly recoil or the air resistance will increase in the barrel and the spear may be shot out of your hand. You may cut your hand on one of the barbs if you are lucky, or the spear may pierce your own body or head if you are unlucky. You may also injure someone else. You should be equipped with a loader in the form of a strong metal lever which can be fitted over the spear. This wing-type loader is about ten centimetres long. The hole in the middle is put over the spear tip and, by exerting pressure with the index and third finger of your right hand, you can press the spear down the barrel more easily than by merely pushing it downwards with the palm of your hand

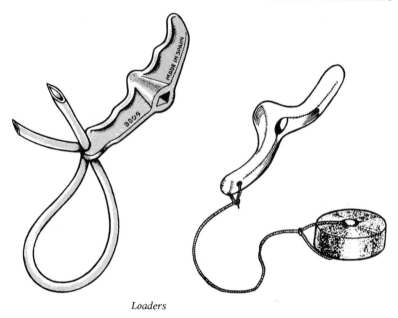

Loaders

or a crumpled glove. The loader should be tied to a cork so that you do not lose it if you drop it in the water.

The loader is a nuisance to carry under water, yet it is indispensable. I place the safety cork inside my swimming trunks at my waist and leave the loader dangling outside. Others tie it to their wrists, and some attach it to a rubber bracelet. Which method you adopt is a matter of personal preference.

THE FISH RING, AND OTHER METHODS
OF CARRYING FISH IN THE WATER

The illustration shows a ring of about twenty centimetres in diameter, which is usually made of steel wire. This ring can be attached to the belt of your bathing trunks or your weight belt— but more of that later. When you have had a successful shot and have taken your fish off your spear, you can save yourself a trip to the shore or your boat and back again to your fishing ground by putting the fish on to a ring. You should open the ring, lead the point of the opened ring wire through the gills so that the wire comes out through the mouth of your fish and then close the ring.

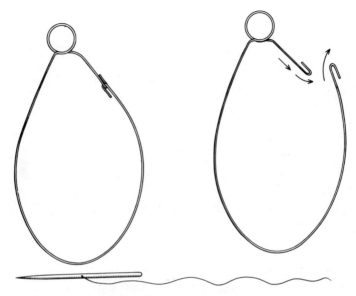

Wire fish ring in closed and open position. Pencil type fish carrier also shown.

If fish are hanging on the ring in this manner even the liveliest of them will be unable to move very much and the rest of your fishing day will not be much disturbed. When you are having a bad day it is a great comfort to glance back at the ring, while swimming along, and see that at least you have caught some fish!

Another way is to have a thick metal pin—say, one centimetre (one quarter of an inch) or less in diameter and about thirty centimetres long with one end sharpened to a point and the other blunt. This pin is attached in the middle to a strongish line which is tied to your belt or dragged through the water. The metal pin and the line form a T. The sharp end is put through the gills and the whole metal bar is then pulled out of the mouth, so that, when the line is pulled, the mouth of the fish comes up against the bar at right angles.

In shark- and barracuda-infested waters it is imperative to fit the fish ring with a float and attach it to a long line so that hungry visitors cannot mistake your fins for one of your flapping victims. In these waters it is perhaps preferable to use the inner tube of a tyre fitted with a strong net below the surface and a net cover above. The fish are then thrown in and the tyre dragged along on the surface but even this should not be less than six metres from your fins.

Nothing, of course, can beat a tireless and enthusiastic girl friend who will follow you in a rowing boat wherever you go, take the fish off your spear, keep them in the boat and render this service the sweeter with a stream of admiring exclamations.

THE KNIFE

It is useful to carry a knife, if possible of stainless steel. There are some on the market with cork handles so that if you drop one while in the water you will not lose it. It can be carried on the belt or in a scabbard fixed on your gun. In spite of aggressive advertising and great care to wash knives with fresh water, they all rust sooner or later.

Many knives come with two straps so that they can be fixed to the calf of your leg. I have a personal prejudice against this. The wearer reminds me of a city-dweller carrying a plastic gun on a dude-ranch.

I carry my knife (sometimes even two knives) on my belt, but some people strap it to their Aqualungs. It is a matter of taste in the last analysis.

People have often asked me what use a knife is under water. I have had the following uses:

(a) A fish is speared inside a rock and cannot be dislodged by pulling at the line and spear. You can go to the other side of the rock and try to pull the fish towards you by hand. It may be impossible to pull the fish out *and* the line *and* the gun. Having fixed the fish and spear between rocks so that it cannot move, you then return to the original side, cut the line and go back to pull out the fish by the head with the loose spear still in it. Remember to retrieve your gun, too.

(b) A fish is speared under a rock and nothing will dislodge it. You have to go to the surface and get another gun and spear the fish in the head through another hole on the other side of the rock. It will then come out easily once you have cut the line of your first gun leaving the original spear to dangle from the fish. Before coming up again do not forget your first gun lying on the ground on the other side of the rock.

(c) It is also an act of mercy to plunge the tip of your knife into the place where you think your captured fish's brain is, and kill it. It will then not attract shark or barracuda by flapping about on your fish ring.

(d) If you have speared a moray eel, you can insert the tip of your knife into its mouth and first cut its upper and then its lower jaw. Even though it is safe, it is not very comfortable, to have a lively moray on your fish ring, even if it is attached to your swimming trunks.

(e) If your gun line gets inextricably tangled with your legs or around a rock, you can cut it with the knife and then pick up your gun.

(f) The metal handle of the knife can be used to attract the attention of other divers in the vicinity by hitting it against a rock or your Aqualung.

(g) Finally, if you see a great white shark, or another great shark or killer whale going straight for you and you are quite certain you cannot escape, pull out your knife quickly and, holding it firmly in your right hand, cut your throat before the attacker gets you. I do not write with any experience on this point.

EARPLUGS AND RUBBER CAPS

Most fishermen will find that their ears begin hurting when they go below a certain depth. This varies with individuals, and each person will react differently every day. For a detailed analysis of the effects of pressure on the ears and other parts of the body, see Chapter 6. Earplugs, earwax or a rubber cap over the ears are of no use whatever and, inasmuch as they impede the easy natural equalization of pressure, they are positively dangerous. Air at surface pressure would be trapped in the outer ear canal between the earplug and the outside of the eardrum. There is no way of changing the pressure of this particular small quantity of air. When you have brought up the pressure on the inside of the eardrum to the level of the lungs by pressing air against your pinched nose, you will have equalized it with the surrounding water. The eardrum could then burst outwards towards the earplug with grave consequences. So I stress that earplugs are not only useless but dangerous.

Hair, when exposed for a long time to sea water, especially if the water is not clean, will become encrusted with salt, plankton, etc. and should be washed frequently. Some spearfishermen wear a rubber cap to keep their hair clean, but I recommend that the ears be kept clear of the cap.

GLOVES, SHIRTS, RUBBER OR NEOPRENE SUITS

In warm climates most people will tend to use only bathing trunks for spearfishing. All that is needed is a pocket for spare spear points and a belt or at least a loop for the line holding the fish ring and the knife. Practice has shown that it is useful to wear gloves on both hands. You are constantly touching rocks or coral, you are handling the spear and the gun, and it is hoped you will handle fish. A pair of cotton gardening gloves or non-slip stevedores' gloves is useful because leather becomes slippery when wet. Unless you are likely to handle larger groupers (French—mérou; Spanish—mero; Italian—cernia) or sharks, you might as well cut the fingertips off or wear something like golfing mittens to leave the tips of your fingers free. It must be remembered that groupers have row upon row of sharp teeth, even inside the gills, and sharks are sharks.

I have sometimes found it useful to wear a knitted cotton or wool shirt or sweater, even in the warmest climates if I am not yet very sunburnt. I am then protected from the strong sun and against cuts and abrasions through contact with rocks or coral.

The Californian and many other waters, even in the summer, are relatively cold, so that many people wear a woollen shirt or even long woollen underwear. Though the woollen garment gets completely wet, it reduces the loss of body heat by keeping in the same quantity of water and a certain amount of air bubbles around the body. Frank Rodecker and Jack Prodanovich, the great California veterans, accompanied me for almost an hour in 1952 in water rather less than fifteen degrees centigrade (sixty degrees Fahrenheit) wearing only trunks. I have no idea how they did it day in and day out. My teeth were chattering and knees shaking for a good half hour after only twenty minutes in the sea.

Even the warmest seas will get uncomfortable after some hours and I have yet to meet a spearfisherman who will not tend to stay in the water longer than is good for him.

There are on the market the rubber suits originally worn by 'frogmen'. They are still rather expensive and need a great deal of care and attention. Full rubber or dry suits such as these must involve the wearing of a great deal of lead on a belt to reduce buoyancy and are thus not to be worn by the beginner. However, you can buy sponge rubber or neoprene vests and trousers which do not keep the water out completely but which achieve more efficient results than woollen garments. They are called wet suits and there are now many good ones on the market. But even here the diver will need more weight on his belt than if he were naked.

THE NOSE CLIP

Nose clips are worn by some people inside the mask covering eyes and nose, to facilitate 'blowing the nose' in the process of clearing the Eustachian tubes. These have become redundant in masks where the nose may be pinched by the thumb and finger from outside the mask.

THE GAFF

I sometimes carry a gaff, attached to my gun but easily removable. It is useful, though very clumsy, when trying to dislodge a big fish which has buried itself in a hole in a rock after being hit.

THE DEPTH GAUGE

A rectangle of plastic with a hole at the side which leads into an air channel in the body of the plastic is the simplest depth gauge available. The sides of the channel are graduated, giving depths in feet or metres. The rectangle is fitted to the wrist. As you descend, water enters into the hole and goes up the channel, compressing the air caught in it. As it continues to compress the air, the border-line between the water and the air gives the reading of the depth.

There are now much more elaborate depth gauges available, but they all work on the same principle. (See page 52.)

THE WRIST-WATCH PROTECTOR AND PRESSURIZED WATCHES

There are several types of metal casing and strong glass protectors for wrist-watches which are helpful to makers of waterproof wrist-

Top left and below right: *Two types of simple and cheap depth gauges to be worn on wrist. Air tunnel open at one end allows water to enter as water pressure increases, compressing the air in the tunnel. The air and water divisions line marks the depth reached. Bottom left: More elaborate and reliable depth gauge which works on same principle. Bottom centre: pressurized compass. Sometimes depth gauge and compass are incorporated in one instrument.*

DEPTH GAUGES

watches in maintaining their reputations, since the usual guarantees do not always cover exposure to four atmospheres of water pressure. But there are now many watches tested to one hundred metres' depth which are quite cheap and in most cases very efficient.

THE WEIGHT BELT

You will very soon find that the human body, especially when a mask and fins are worn, is buoyant in water—particularly salt water.

Practical weight belt. The half kilo lead weights easily slide on and off the belt which has one simple end that slides through buckle.

Weight belts, able to carry several kilogrammes of lead weights, have now been on the market for many years.

You should test yourself with various weights until you are gently sinking. Novices, however, should become proficient at everything treated in this book before they try weight belts.

I have found the best weights to be those of half a kilogramme (one pound) each, which can be put on or taken off the belt while it is still in position. The next best are weights which can be easily slid on and off the loose end of the belt once it has been taken off the body.

I have found many types of weight belt available 'for the birds' except the fairly wide one which has a simple aircraft safety belt buckle on one end through which the other loose end is slipped and the buckle clipped down. If you dive in groups it is better to have your belt of a distinctive colour or with a plastic identity disc to avoid waste of time or quarrels.

COMPASS

When diving with an Aqualung in deep water far from the shore it is useful to have a pressurized compass on your wrist, and to learn how to use it from the various books available.

THERMOMETER

There are on the market pressurized thermometers. I always forget to look at mine!

TORCHES

There are now many pressurized torches on the market. Their use for night diving is obvious, but even in daytime I have many times flashed my torch into caves and holes and found fish I would not otherwise have seen.

CAMERAS, FILM EQUIPMENT, EQUIPMENT FOR RAIDING WRECKS AND FOR ARCHAEOLOGY

Many books have been written on these subjects but they have no place in my book which is devoted to beginners under water.

As a guide, however, I want to mention the works of Dimitri Rebikoff, the pioneer in this field, the Italian magazine *Mondo Sommerso*, and the American magazine *Skin Diver*. Also the following books: *Underwater Photography* by Jerry Greenberg, *Beginning Underwater Photography* by Jim and Cathy Church and *Beginner's Guide to Photography Under Water* by Ron Church. These books are obtainable from Aqua-Craft, 5258 Anna St, San Diego, California 92110, though *Beginning Underwater Photography* is available in Great Britain.

DIVER'S FLAG

The diver's flag, a red square with a thick white diagonal line, flown on a rowing boat, rubber dinghy or a mere float, has now been accepted generally to show that there are divers in the immediate vicinity. Those driving other craft in such waters are begged to watch out.

LIFE JACKETS

There are now several makes of inflatable life jackets on the market. Even when not inflated, their buoyancy involves extra lead on the weight belt.

Many people think that, once inflated, the life jacket will enable a tired spearfisherman to reach the shore more easily. I find them a nuisance. It is far safer, both in ordinary diving and diving with an Aqualung, to have a man in a rowing boat or with an outboard motor follow the diver or divers very closely. Many people cannot afford this, but it is far better to team up with others and have a boat than to have to rely on a clumsy journey back, swimming with an inflated life jacket. I have found, even in an emergency, that swimming or floating with just a mask and fins is far less tiring. The head, with air in the mask, is easily supported by the water. With the head out of the water (inevitable with an inflated lifebelt), floating and waiting for help with the feet dangling below is very tiring.

Anyone who really and truly *must* have a lifebelt as an emergency safety measure is simply not a good enough swimmer—nor relaxed enough in the water—to be doing anything else than hugging the shore where only a few strokes would achieve safety.

AQUALUNG PRESSURE GAUGE

There are some of these, attachable to the Aqualung and advertised as a safety measure. As you should never dive deep until you have learnt to recognize when your air supply is low and start coming up, this device is redundant.

With all this equipment you are now quite ready to start spearfishing. Breathing may prove the most difficult task to master. At the beginning you will find that something will go wrong all the time. Either you will not be able to breathe because water has entered your mask, or you will not be able to see through your mask because the additional pressure below the surface has caused your mask to change position and water has entered the mask.

You have to learn how to put your mask on properly and you will have to learn how to swim holding the spear or gun in your hand. You should also learn to swim with your legs only. It may sometimes be necessary for you to hold heavy guns in both hands when cruising along the surface.

You will find that many days will pass before you will feel at ease and can begin enjoying your spearfishing, so, unless you have a very long holiday, you have very little time left for the sport.

It is fortunately possible to do most of your preparatory work and your training at home. You can go through all the preliminary stages in a swimming pool.

The very first thing to do is to learn to use your mask. You must accustom yourself to movement in every direction at varying speeds and depths with your mask on. When you feel quite comfortable with your mask over your eyes, you can then begin to use whichever snorkel you have chosen, unless, of course, you have begun practising with a mask incorporating a snorkel. You can then accustom yourself to using fins on your feet. You should soon reach the stage of moving about the swimming pool with your mask over your face, using your snorkel quite freely, being able to swim about the pool with your fins and being able to hold your breath under water. Then try diving in the pool as described in Chapter 4.

You will find that everything under water is enlarged when seen through your mask. A good way to accustom yourself to movement and judging distances and angles under water is to drop coins to the bottom of the swimming pool and then try to pick them up. I should then try the same thing wearing a woollen garment, a knife, a fish ring, and gloves, and only then with a weight belt.

I do not know how many swimming pools will let you practise with a spear or gun. You may be able to arrange to have the swimming pool to yourself or at the disposal of a group at certain hours. In that case I should advise you to construct a target in the form of a fish not longer than eighteen centimetres. This 'fish' can be made of wood or cork, and should be attached by a string to a heavy object such as a stone or a piece of metal. You then drop your target into the middle of the pool. If the string is about sixty centimetres long, you will find that your target will appear to be a fish hovering at this distance from the bottom of your swimming pool. Try approaching your target from quite a distance and shooting at it from different angles and at all sorts of ranges. If you get a friend to help you, you will probably be able to invent a kind of moving underwater target by using a tin 'fish' suspended from a line and a pole, with your friend walking along the side of the pool. You must, of course, use some kind of padding over the point of your spear in order not to damage the swimming pool!

By the time you have become a decent shot at a target which is quite still, and have learned to load your gun in the water in the manner described in Chapter 4, you will have achieved a considerable degree of efficiency in moving under the water equipped with some or all the paraphernalia mentioned. You are ready now to take a holiday and go after the real thing.

4

THE TECHNIQUE OF SPEARFISHING

Nec semper feriet quodcumque minibitur arcus.
(Not always will the bolt hit that at which it is
aimed.) HORACE
De Arte Poetica

Who cannot catch fish must catch shrimps.
(Chinese Proverb)

Let us assume that you are now at ease in the water. You are able
to move about quite freely on and below the surface with your
mask on, your snorkel in your mouth, your fins on your feet and
your spear gun in your hand. Let us assume also that you have
chosen your ground and that you are therefore ready and longing
to go after real fish.

ENTERING THE SEA

You must not forget to bring a towel and spare bathing trunks
with you. You will find that if you have spent about an hour or so
even in the warmest water you will be cold when you come out.

I must also add that if you are swimming in the Mediterranean
in the summer, or in any other sunny climate, you should not start
spearfishing unless you have become sunburned. As you swim
along the surface of the water you are exposing part of your back
constantly to the sun, while the rest of it is submerged. This is the
surest way of getting a burn—five minutes exposed to the sun in
such circumstances is equivalent to at least a quarter of an hour of
sunbathing on the beach.

Choose a place very near the edge of the water in order to avoid
having to walk over rocks with your fins on. Even the fittest

athlete feels like a clumsy old duck walking over rocks with fins on his feet. Make a careful note of the place where you have left your towel and other equipment, so that when you are in the water and wish to come back you do not have to search a long time for your landing place. Your field of vision is not very wide when your mask is on, and after an hour's strenuous diving you will be in no mood to search about the coast for your landing place, whether you are handling a successful catch or not. If possible, choose a spot from which you will be able to wade into the water without having to dive. This is also important for your return.

I used to advise beginners to load their guns out of the water first and apply the safety catch. No really satisfactory safety catch has yet been devised for spearfishing guns. I think it safer for the beginner not to rely on safety catches at all but to learn to take care all the time. After all, you only save yourself one loading in the water and if you miss as often as I do, you will load your gun many times on each outing.

Check your reel, if you have one, and also the position of your line. Then place the gun and spear near the edge of the water, with the line clear, so that you can pick them up on your way in. The next thing to do is to sit down on the ground, keeping as near to the edge of the water as you can, and put on your fins. You will find it best to wet your feet and the fins before you put them on. Then, tie your fish ring to your belt on your left flank. The knife, if it is not fixed to your calf or your gun, should be carried on the left side too. Your watch and your depth gauge should already be on your wrist and your loader attached to your body. When you have done all this and put your gloves on, you are ready for your mask, making sure a mist will not form on the inside of the glass. Once the mask is on and your snorkel is in your mouth, you are ready to go into the water.

All this is much easier if you are in a boat or a dinghy, because everything is handy and the water is deep enough to allow you to lower yourself overboard carefully without making a splash.

If you have to go into the water from the shore by jumping in, your mask will probably come off (unless you have jumped in backwards), you may lose your gun, or you may make a splash which will frighten the fish that happen to be near. It is therefore best to try and launch yourself into the water from a crouching position in much the same way as an elderly dowager would enter the water from the steps of a swimming pool if she wished to avoid getting her face and hair wet.

You must be careful to avoid stepping on the black sea urchins that dot so many coasts. You should try to begin swimming as soon as the water is more than knee-deep to avoid touching the sea urchins with your feet. The prickles of a sea urchin break off more easily than a hedgehog's and are difficult to extract, although they will do you little harm beyond causing discomfort.

Just before a shot is taken. The rubber pipes have not yet been cocked. Note that the author wears a knife at the back of his belt.
Photograph by Eric Weinmann

If you must go into the water at a beach where fairly strong waves are breaking, you must already have your fins on your feet, knife attached to your belt, calf or gun, mask on, and gun in your right hand. Your spear should also be carried in your right palm, with the line at its shortest. Wade in, walking sideways as though you were a skier trying to go downhill with skis on but not skiing.

This way the left side of your body is exposed to the breakers rather than the front where you could be winded by a blow. A stage will be reached where you are before the actual line of the breakers. Turn quickly and face the waves, hold the gun and spear firmly and closely to your side and, as the breaking wave approaches, lower your head to protect the glass of your mask and lunge forward into the wave, having taken a deep breath first. With luck, you are through the barrier, but you may have to repeat this once or twice going steadily forwards. By this time crouch and keep your feet lightly on the ground so that as little as possible of you is exposed to the full force of the water.

STALKING

Once in the water, load your gun (in the manner I shall describe later), pause and look around you. Start swimming slowly along the surface of the water, making as little of a splash with your fins as you can, looking forward and below you, turning your head to the left and to the right from time to time.

At all times when you are handling the gun in the water be extremely careful not to point it at anybody. It is a lethal weapon. If you have any doubt about my warning, go to a place out in the air where you are by yourself, detach the line from your spear and shoot at a tree trunk, and you will see the speed of the spear and the distance it will cover.

At first sight it may appear to you that there are no fish at all in the neighbourhood, but as soon as your eyes have accustomed themselves to the surroundings you will begin to notice fish. If you see more than one which might prove to be a likely target, try to make up your mind which one you will stalk as there will be no time to decide once you are below the surface. You will discover very soon that most fish appear to hear extremely well. The movements you make while swimming are to them the movements of a strange monster. If you splash about or make a noise with your breathing, you will find it very difficult to get near any of them. (It is immaterial here whether the fish hear you or feel the vibrations caused by you on their skins.) Pause from time to time and lie quite still, just keeping yourself afloat. After a little practice you will be able to do this by means of a very small movement of your free hand and by very slow movements of your fins in the fashion of

Simple dive

the crawl stroke. In the illustrations on these pages you will see the manner in which you should carry your gun and dive towards your fish. At every moment of the dive you must move smoothly, trying again to imitate a fish. Try and pause in your dive. Remember that the slower your movements are and the slower your dive is, the lower is the rate of your oxygen consumption. Contrary to your instinct, therefore, take as long as you can to go down, move about the bottom in slow motion and come up slowly. By the time you are in position A, shown in the illustrations of the angle and vertical dives, you should have made up your mind which fish you will go for. You should not take your eyes off your fish while you are executing movement B, which consists of bending at the waist and pointing your head downwards. There are two ways of executing stage B. One is, as I have said, to bend at the waist as if you were making a deep bow, then to use your free hand in an

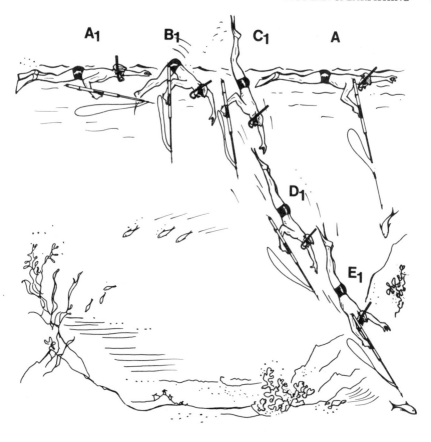

upward movement to push yourself down when the fins are under water. It is more satisfactory, however, to lower yourself under water vertically until your snorkel is submerged. Then, only when your snorkel is below the surface should you execute movement B. The time you are most likely to make a noise with splashing fins is when you try to execute the movement shown in position C. Therefore do not begin moving your feet until both feet and the entire surface of the fins are below the water.

There are two main ways of executing a dive. The first, as illustrated, is to dive towards the fish at a relatively easy angle

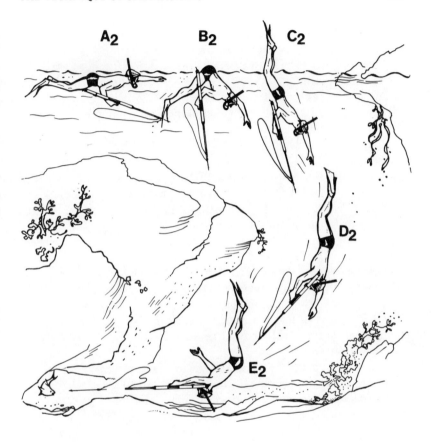

which will enable you to reach your fish without having to twist your head. Because of the angle, you will naturally cover a longer distance to your target than the actual vertical depth. The advantage of this method of diving is that you do not take your eye off the target and you can, if necessary, execute turns to the left or right on your way down.

The second method, also illustrated, shows a vertical dive. It has the advantage of a shorter distance and of a method of approach to a fish which makes the advent of the hunter almost unnoticed until the very last moment. This may involve shooting from an upside-down position and completely turning your body below in order to come up again. Changing direction in a vertical dive is not as easy or as effective as during an angle dive.

Jack Ackerman of Hawaii was already a vertical diver in 1952. His manœuvrability under water was tremendous. Having learned to dive at an angle, I found it uncomfortable to execute vertical dives at first, in spite of much encouragement from him. I was soon accustomed to this method too.

I would recommend beginners to practise both methods from the start.

José Beltrán of Majorca, when I first met him in 1950, was one of Spain's most famous early spearfishermen. He dived vertically and his great feat then was to dive without fins. He felt they prevented him from twisting and turning freely among rocks and claimed that diving down doing a vertical breast stroke was a more silent and more cautious approach than using fins. I found that he could get down to depths of between ten and fifteen metres with me quite easily. I got there first even with an angle dive but using my fins. His lung capacity was much greater than mine so that he gained on me below what he lost coming down. Finally I gave him a Hans Hass model pair of fins and after that he manufactured and used his own until his retirement.

It is worth recording Jack Ackerman's magnificent technique in stalking pompano. He may still hold the world's record of fifty-eight kilogrammes speared in the summer of 1953. Pompano are a very fast open-sea fish. It is virtually impossible to get near enough to spear them in the open sea. They come in to stalk smaller fish in deep rocky caves along the petrified lava shore of the Hawaiian Islands. They seem to prefer localities where two adjacent caves, joined by a passage under water, give them an escape route and at the same time give them a greater chance of surprising their own intended victims. The larger pompano will frequent caves where the sheer rocky sides go to depths of at least twenty metres. Ackerman will spot a pair of caves, make me place myself at the entrance of one, and he will go to the other. At a shout from him we both dive and plan to meet at either end of the passage between the caves. The instant a pompano is spotted it must be shot at. If we are lucky, we heave into sight near the fish. Otherwise, its lightning speed will give us no chance. If there is only one cave, Ackerman will sportingly approach the base at the shore side, leaving me to stay at the wider entrance to the cave. A vertical dive by him will scare the pompano out of their hiding place towards the open sea, by which time I am theoretically down at fifteen metres waiting to hit them as they flash by. This method is only possible when the whole system of rocks forming the cave reaches out of the sea, allowing the 'beater' to dive vertically to the base of the cave from the side without being seen by the fish. This technique is possible in all seas where open-sea fish occasionally come to the shore to feed.

In Chapter 2, I described various spearfishing grounds, but more should be said about stalking in different places.

In the opinion of the late Dr Gianni Roghi, one of the most celebrated and experienced early spearfishermen in Italy (which has some of the best spearfishermen anywhere) the ideal number for team stalking is three. A greater number loading and firing, moving about in all directions and diving on exploratory work will cause the timid fish to fly away and rock-dwelling fish to retreat into the safety of deeper holes. To avoid shouting and lifting one's head above water or treading water with fins—all actions unnatural to the inhabitants of the sea and thus disturbing to them—a system of signs should be agreed on in advance. Dr Roghi advised the following technique for a rocky shore. The three men move along a shore. Suppose they think they may find a group of likely victims at the base or in the middle of a cove. Fisherman A, nearest the shore, should quietly continue to near the entrance of the cove and wait out of sight of any possible fish in the cove. Fisherman B should make an arc and approach the middle of the mouth of the cove while fisherman C, who was swimming furthest from the shore, should make the greatest arc and place himself at the other side of the cove in a position corresponding to A. The first dive should be given to B. Whether he is successful with his own shot or not, he will at all events scatter the group, and if A and C remain out of sight at their posts, the fish will not swim away into the open at lightning speed but will try to move off, not too far, always in the hope of rejoining their group when that monster B has gone. This is the moment when A and C go into their dives, each at his end of the cove entrance.

In the open sea it is also possible to surround a fish by having A and C describe large arcs while the victim's attention is centred on the slowly and directly approaching B. This technique is suitable for all open-sea or migratory fish such as barracuda, amberjack, sea wolf or white bass, dentex, golden sea bream. (See Chapter 8 for a detailed description of the more common fishes.)

I have also found with these open-sea fishes that if I rolled myself into more or less a ball shape, holding my knees as near my chin as possible with my arms and allowing myself to sink gently, these fish were sometimes curious and courageous enough to come quite near. A sudden lunge turns me once again into a spearfisherman.

If the rocky shore is steep, it is best to follow near the shore. The distance from the rocks will depend on the state of the sea. If it is calm you can swim at a metre or so from the rocks, but if the sea is rough it will not be possible to be too near. The foam created by the sea pounding the rocks will reduce visibility almost to nothing. But some distance below the waves the water will be relatively calm and if you see a grouper or another kind of rock-dwelling fish along the steep wall of the shore you may be sure it is not far from its hole. Move very steadily until you are within diving distance and dive sideways along the rock with your shooting arm on the sea side, if at all possible. Even if the fish has gone into its hole, it is almost dead certain that the first thing it will want to do upon entering is to turn around and be ready to peer out. This is the moment to shoot. If he has gone in deeper, give him a little time and dive coming upon the hole suddenly, ready to shoot.

If you see any of the fish that are not proper rock-dwelling fish but which nevertheless frequent rock and are familiar with a fairly wide rocky area, such as croakers or striped sea breams or fish related to them such as snapper in seas outside the Mediterranean, follow them carefully and steadily. Sooner or later they will be frightened by your movements into dashing for cover. Except for the snappers, they never go deep into holes and do not seem happy there. You can then dive and try to hit one while it is moving about quickly under its rock. A rock will often have several entrances. It is best to try another entrance and not the one the fish has entered.

The stalking technique among large rocks below the surface is much the same, except that you need to do many turns and must range your gaze in many directions all the time. While ascending after a dive, keep turning to get the best view of the situation about you.

Grey mullets and similar fish tend to go into shallow water. You will find them where whitish round stones (which get smaller as

A splendid Mediterranean catch.
Photograph by Roberto Dei

you near the shore) may indicate a source of fresh water. They will, unlike the others described above, frequently change direction if frightened. If you approach them from the sea, coming in at right angles to the shore, you can prevent them from going too far to the left or too far to the right. When you have made them change direction two or three times and come almost within shooting distance, they will dive under a rock in despair. This is your chance. Frequently, they will allow themselves to be cornered in a hole in such shallow water that you will be unable to dive and you may not even be able to swim in a foot of water. The same fish over sand, a little deeper and away from the shore, is almost impossible to catch. Barracuda behave in much the same way but, being cleverer, they will make a dash for the open water and safety much sooner.

The stalking technique over a sandy bottom is the same as in the open sea. Here, apart from pure luck, team effort is the only way of cornering a fast-moving, wary, open-sea fish. Fishermen A and C should describe large arcs, one on each side, while the potential victim's attention is centred on the slowly and directly approaching B.

The element of luck may come in the case of all open-sea fish. I have mentioned the trick of rolling yourself into a ball. These fish especially if they are big and if you keep quite still, are curious enough to come a long way to inspect you. If you are lucky and do not need to do much of a turn to shoot, you might get quite a large one. It will probably be necessary to go below the surface to shoot. You can also just lower yourself, as you are and with your head uppermost, to a depth where your head is well below the the surface, and hold your breath for as long as you can. If you must come up for air, do so very slowly. Any sudden movement will tell the fish you are something alive and in a flash it will be gone.

There are two main kinds of coral reefs. The first form islands or patches in an area where the bottom is coral sand. You should swim slowly along the outside edges of the islands where the coral rock will be biggest. Look for places where smaller fish have collected and you should soon find something worth while.

The other coral reefs are the barrier kind. The coral forms a continuous barrier at a certain distance from the shore. In places where there are considerable tides, the lagoon between the shore and the reef edge will be very shallow at times. Then suddenly, where the waves break, you know that there is a steep drop into deep water. Go along this steep barrier as along any rocky shore, being careful to watch the breakers all the time and paying attention to undertow and drift.

If you are on your first visit to coral reefs, having previously fished in the Mediterranean or other Northern waters, you will be much occupied during your first dives in identifying all the multi-coloured cousins of the species you may already know. Thereafter it is a matter of applying the appropriate stalking technique.

In all dives, except where you are invisible to your victim, it is extremely important to move smoothly and, if possible, to pause from time to time without any movement. I believe even looking away, pretending not to be stalking, is helpful, though this may be an illusion.

In many waters there are strong currents pushing much water through narrow channels. I have let myself be carried by these swift currents, followed by a boat with an outboard motor. All you can do then is to look far ahead and dive in time, shooting as you flash over a fish petrified by your fast dive. You cannot turn or go back, but it is great fun. You must be an experienced and strong swimmer to get yourself out of the current back into the calm water by gradually edging out of the current, and you would be foolish to try this game without an experienced seaman in the boat.

SHOOTING TECHNIQUE

On pages 62–3 I have illustrated two of the most common executions of the dive and the position for shooting from the surface (A). The sequence of positions for the dives A1 and A2 can easily be followed from the illustration.

There are some general points which must first of all be mentioned.

Whenever possible you should try to shoot your spear by extending your arm as far as possible, as though you were shooting with a revolver. With guns which have long barrels you can achieve additional comfort by resting on your shoulder that part of the barrel which extends behind the handle and which holds the compressed spring or air. There is also a shorter type of gun with the elastic rubber propulsion method which has a strong metal bracelet around it. This bracelet is fixed over your shooting arm in order to provide additional security and a stronger grip. In all these cases, therefore, you gain something by extending your arm at the time of the shooting.

Very often, however, you may have to shoot more or less suddenly without having a proper opportunity to take aim, and in addition to this, you yourself may be moving at that time. In such a case you should judge your aim as best you can, much in the same way that we have all seen cowboys shoot from the hip in films.

The next thing to bear in mind is that the glass on your mask, coupled with the effect of looking through water, enlarges all objects that you see. This means that you are never quite as near to anything as you may think you are.

You will find that you share the most common fault of all beginners, which is to shoot often and to shoot from too far away. When you have had some experience, you will see that most fish, even when they are being pursued, pause for brief instants to look around. That is the time to fire.

If you have found that your quarry has disappeared under a rock, try to approach the rock from another side. You may thus have a chance of surprising your fish by coming in from an entirely different direction. When you have had some experience in stalking fish, endeavouring to surprise them and generally trying to use your intelligence to corner your quarry, you will realize that fish are by no means stupid.

I have also found that if you approach a rock-dwelling fish outside its home with the sun directly behind you and you plunge down towards it, much in the same way that dive bombers used to come down in the War with the sun behind them, you will stand a far greater chance of getting your fish. If you come towards the fish from the other side with the sun shining on your skin and your trunks, and the gun glistening in the sunlight, you are likely to be seen from far off even by the most myopic fish.

You should try to avoid firing at a fish which is located so near that it is almost touching a rock, because if you miss the fish you will probably hit the rock with your spear and damage its point. Even if you have plenty of spare points, you may regret this because a much bigger fish will swim quietly by while you are struggling to reload your gun or replacing the spear point. Try and spear the fish by firing almost parallel to the rock.

Let us now make a brief analysis of the circumstances in which you may find yourself at the moment of shooting.

VARIATIONS DEPENDING ON THE POSITION OF THE FISHERMAN

1. The Horizontal Shot. You have got yourself into the position where you are lying horizontally under the water at a certain depth. Your body is in the usual swimming position. Your right arm and your gun are therefore along the same axis as your body.

This is the easiest type of shot since your body is being kept level and stationary by the use of your free arm and your two legs. You can achieve almost perfect stability and therefore the precision of your shot should be at its best. You must remember, however, that in this position the force of gravity on your spear will tend to make you shoot low. You must get as near as possible to your target.

2. The Half Dive. Here you will not go deep and you will have plenty of air in your lungs. In such cases you will most probably be firing at your fish while you are still moving a little, although you should try and pause for the instant of firing if you possibly can. If you are moving, this tends to make your shooting much more difficult because you are not in a state of balance. The thing to remember is to maintain the position of your spear or gun so that it is, as far as possible, merely an extension of your body along the same axis. If you have dived and expect only then to put the spear or gun into the shooting position, you will never succeed in doing everything you need to do in the time at your disposal. The moment you have decided to go for a fish you must extend your arm so that everything is ready for the moment when you let go of your spear or pull the trigger. As you are plunging down towards your fish you may very well have to twist to the left or to the right, and you may even have to turn. During all this time be careful to keep your spear straight in front of you and along the same axis as your body. And remember to relax and move slowly.

3. The Deep Dive. You may arrive at the sea bed, whatever its depth below the surface may be, and you will have to fire at a fish which may be resting under a rock or just turning a corner or grazing along the bottom. By the time you have arrived at the bottom you are handicapped by the feeling that your air supply will not last very much longer. Your aim may not be so good because you will not have time to get your head and arm in the position which comes easiest to you for aiming and firing. You must be careful in such circumstances not to let the point of your spear go too far in front of your eye. The arrival of your spear within the fish's range of vision without your eye and your arm being ready to aim and shoot will only cause the fish to disappear from view. At a time when your brain informs you that you need

fresh air you are not likely to feel that you have sufficient time to
aim quietly and shoot. Therefore get yourself to the fish in such a
state that you can shoot instantly and take your chance. This means
a slow dive and pinching your nose all the time. Nowadays, in the
Mediterranean young men have to make a deep dive every time
to about twenty metres even if they have not seen a fish, but just
to inspect a deep rock.

VARIATIONS DEPENDING ON THE POSITION OF THE FISH

There are six principal positions in which the fish may offer itself
as a target.

1. The Broadside Position. You and your quarry are on the same
horizontal plane. You may turn clockwise or counter-clockwise
but still on this horizontal plane, depending upon the movement
of the fish. If you can wait till the moment when the fish exposes
its broadside to you, you will have the target in its best position.
You should take into account the speed at which the fish is swimming and try to fire a little bit forward of its head, much in the
same way that you would shoot at a bird. If you have also managed
to come sufficiently near, you will have achieved the ideal shooting
position.

2. The Fish Faces the Fisherman. Some fish prefer to keep away
from rocks and from vegetation and are generally of the wandering
type. You will only run across them in the open sea. Such fish
should not be pursued because you will never catch them, but it
is at times worth while to keep as still as possible and wait for the
fish to approach you. You will soon observe, wherever you happen
to be and whatever the particular species of fish you encounter in
such circumstances, that these lone fellows are much braver than
other fish. They will be inclined to approach you themselves and
even swim around and examine you as though they were trying
to discover what on earth this strange-looking object was. You
must not even point your gun at them, but try and keep as still as
you possibly can, making very slow and surreptitious movements
with your hands and your legs in order to get yourself in the
position to shoot. It is extremely unlikely that such a fish will

ever offer its broadside to you, but you may find it approaching the point of your spear and coming quite near. You therefore have to shoot at the fish head on. Your only chance of getting it on to your spear in such cases is to shoot at the head. By the time your spear point has made contact, you will probably find that you have hit the fish broadside on anyway.

3. When only the Fish's Back is Visible. You are directly above the fish, and, try as you might, you cannot get yourself into the horizontal aiming position or anything away from the vertical. The best advice in such cases is not to shoot at all, but if the fish is really big enough you may find it impossible to resist the temptation and, indeed, the larger the fish the more likely you are to hit it as you have a larger surface exposed to your weapon. The only fish which are easy to shoot coming down upon them vertically and with a chance of success are soles and related types. Rays also belong to this category, but I should class them among dangerous fish for the beginner.

4. Where only the Soft Underbelly is Visible. Such cases are exceptional. You will very rarely be in a fit state when you are rising up from the bottom, even if you do see a fish above you, to try and make even a passable shot. I should say that the only fish worth having a shot at in such cases are rays and, with exceptional luck, some of the larger open-sea fish.

5. The Fish Either Faces You or is Swimming Away but is Showing about Three-quarters of its Body. This is the position you will come across most frequently. You will find a fish down at the bottom, perhaps looking at you or perhaps turned away from you, and as you dive towards it you may find that it remains quite still. But when you have come near enough you may suddenly find it will shift its position. If you then try and make a turn in order to improve your angle so that you have a larger surface of its body visible to you, you will be exasperated to find that by almost imperceptible movements the fish has remained facing you, or if it was originally turned from you, it may still be ready for flight. Do not hesitate to shoot if you are reasonably near and the body of the fish is at an angle with the direction of your movement of more than forty-five degrees. By the time you have found a better position, you will probably be much too short of air to do anything else but come up to the surface again.

6. Groupers. Groupers come under a special category. By the time you reach a reasonably-sized grouper, he will be under a rock poised for a brief second facing you. It is now or never and you must shoot at his head from straight in front, as illustrated. If you hit a grouper anywhere else the chances are that he will go deep into his rock and wedge himself in. Only a tremendous struggle will unhinge this brave animal after that.

Here I must enter a general defence for shooting at non-moving fish, a practice unthinkable with birds or land animals. A fish which is quite still is in fact at its most alert. Your weapon is the equivalent of an extremely inefficient arrow on land, and not of a gun which spreads shot over a wide area.

A fish that has been speared will not be able to get very far, unless it is rather large and strong. Even if you have lost your fish, try and follow it with your eyes during the time that you are coming up for air and while you are on the surface reloading your gun. With average luck you should be able to spear it at the second attempt and start the laborious process of 'landing' your catch.

You should aim to spear your fish in the most vital parts. In the accompanying illustrations I have shown where you should aim. Even if you have succeeded only in making a bad shot, according to my illustrations, you may still have a very good chance of landing your catch. You must avoid hitting the fore part of the head which is usually the hardest part of the fish, as your spear may not pierce through the skin and bone, unless you are shooting at a grouper or another type of rockfish which should, if possible, be hit in the head from the front as described. The parts of the fish marked by diagonal lines are those which are softest. If you have speared your fish in those areas you may find that the flesh is simply torn away, and the fish has swum off, wounded but free.

Try to follow the rule of never letting a wounded fish get away to suffer the agonies of a slow death. The narrow part of the tail just ahead of the caudal fin is in fact an extremely important centre of its swimming equipment. I have marked it as a bad shot, but if you in fact spear your fish just there you will probably manage to keep it.

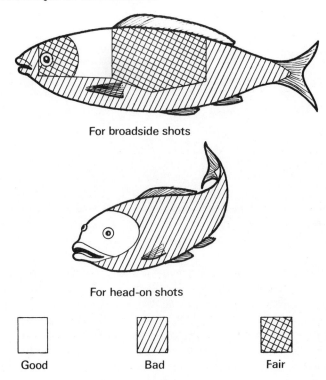

For broadside shots

For head-on shots

Good   Bad   Fair

AFTER TAKING THE SHOT

Let us assume that you have missed your fish at your first attempt. The spear, if it is attached to your gun, will shoot past the fish, and perhaps hit a rock or perhaps gradually fall to the bottom. The first thing is to remember to keep holding your gun. If you use a simple sea-lance, hold on to it. Turn your head upwards, get your body into the vertical position and propel yourself to the surface of the water. Bring back your spear by using your reel or pull in your line by hand and then load your gun again in the manner which I shall describe later. If you can manage it, keep your eyes on the fish you have just missed so that you may have another try in a minute. Before you reach the surface, look up to see that your way to it is clear and that you will not hit a rock or get involved in kelp on your way up. Once your gun has been reloaded you are ready to start again.

'LANDING' YOUR CATCH

If, on the other hand, you have managed to strike your fish, the first thing to remember is to get hold of your line with your free hand as soon as you can, in order to prevent the fish from swimming away too far or hiding under a rock. If you allow either of these things to happen you may find great difficulty in getting your spear back without damaging it. Most spears are made of an aluminium-steel alloy and are easily bent if they get stuck between rocks and you try to pull too hard. The great thing, therefore, is to prevent your speared fish from hiding under a rock. If you can manage to keep it in the open water so that it is not within reach of any rock or vegetation, you will find that, unless it is large, it will not be in a position to struggle too hard.

Try and pull your line in so that you can get your hand on the spear. The first thing to do then is to try and get hold of the fish by the head if it is small or place the index finger in one eye and the thumb in the other, or even to put a finger in its mouth and hold it close to your body. Push the spear through the body of the fish so that the winged barbs come out on the other side. With the winged barbs against its flesh on the other side, the fish cannot get away. Even so, hold on to the fish close to your body or hold the spear in both hands, one on each side of the fish. With a big fish you must remember (if you have not killed it dead with your shot) that it will not pull hard at first. It is stunned, surprised and, presumably, hurt. Only when you have made contact with the spear with your hand will it realize that it is in real trouble. Then the struggle begins. You must prevent it from pulling at your spear so hard that it will pull it out of your hand. If it starts swimming in circles and all you have to hold on to is your gun, it becomes very difficult for you to swim back to the surface. Rather than to try to swim to the surface against this tremendous pull, you should dive down again (in the same breath, of course) and pull yourself to the fish, grabbing the spear again and the fish as well. By that time don't worry about my advice to ram the spear through the fish holding the spear from both sides. Grab the fish and embrace it like a long lost child. On your way up try to remember to ram the spear through, but go on hugging the fish. I have lost many a larger amberjack by forgetting my own advice in the excitement and for lack of breath.

By the time you have done all this you will have developed an earnest desire to come back to the surface before doing anything else. Once you are up at the surface the most important thing is to get your breath back and to take a brief rest. The rest need only be for a few seconds. Keep quite still for a moment, breathe slowly and deeply. Remember never to drop your gun. Some guns have a clip at the butt by means of which you can attach them to the belt of your trunks, so that both your arms may be free for what follows. But for heaven's sake do not use this method with a big fish at the other end of your line. It is better to go on holding your gun in one hand.

In the case of a small fish, bring your spear up by the use of your reel or by pulling in your line by hand, so that you can get hold of it with your free hand. If the fish is not on properly and you have not done what I have just advised you must pull your line in, gingerly but swiftly, without using the reel which is slow.

You may find it quite difficult to get your fish off the spear. Get hold of it very firmly by the gills by inserting the thumb of your left hand under one gill and at least your index finger under the other. Then adjust the movable barbs on your harpoon so that by clipping them down flush with the point you can slide the fish off, still holding the fish firmly by the thumb and index finger of your left hand. Continue holding the spear with your right hand. This means that you must hold your gun under your right arm or between your knees. With your two hands thus occupied, and if the gun is between your knees, you have, of course, nothing with which to swim, so you will find that you start sinking. Do not worry about that, but take a deep breath and continue the process while you are holding your breath and slowly sinking. Now, take your gun in your right hand again. You are now holding the spear and the gun in your hand. Still firmly holding the gills of the fish with your left hand, come up for air again. If you want to make quite sure that you will not lose the gun, wind the line two or three times round your right hand. Thus, even if by some mischance you drop your gun, you will not have lost it. If you like to make things easier for yourself, swim to a place where it is relatively shallow and drop the gun there. But there is a better way. Before you try to slip the fish off your spear, open your fish ring. Then lead the wire point through the gills so that it comes out through the mouth and clip the wire of the fish ring together. Only then slip the fish off the spear. It is perhaps better to have the fish ring suspended from your belt by a line about sixty centimetres long so that you can perform the operation of leading the wire point through the gills by holding the fish in front of your eyes, instead of doing this with the fish ring tied closely to your left hip. At all times keep the fish ring on your left flank, so that it does not catch on to your gun or get tangled with your line, both of which you will have on your right flank, when swimming or shooting. When slipping the fish off the spear, you must make sure that the whole fish is under the water because if you take it out of the water and into the air it will start struggling wildly and you may lose it. You should also keep it under the water while you are putting it on your fish ring.

The technique for taking the fish off the spear if you have to unscrew the spear point to enable the fish to come off is as follows. Slip the fish down the spear. Hold the spear upright, keeping the fish below your hand, unscrew the point and then get hold of the fish by the gills with either hand, still holding on to your point in the palm of one hand (pity you cannot hold the spear point in your mouth like a good needlewoman). Put the fish on the ring, then slip it off the spear and screw the point back. It is safer, however, to put the fish on to your ring before unscrewing the spear point.

Then unwind the line from your right hand, and you are ready to load your gun again with the fish safely on your ring.

All these operations sound wildly complicated, and let me assure you that while you are trying to breathe and at the same time to keep afloat without the use of your arms and legs, they are indeed very complicated. There are so many things which can go wrong in the general excitement which accompanies a successful spearing that you may have many opportunities at the beginning to come back ashore and tell your story of how that big fish got away.

LOADING THE GUN

Whether your shot has been successful or not, you have to face the problem of loading your gun again.

However difficult you may find it at first, it is absolutely necessary for you to load the gun in the water. Otherwise you will have to come back to the shore or your boat every time you have fired and your fishing day will be spent swimming back and forth to

How to take fish photographs. It is always advisable to hold the fish as far forward as possible and with little children present, preferably babies!
Photograph by Eric Weinmann

and from the place where you load your gun, and this may mean great distances and much exertion.

The loading position, both for guns which work on the principle of the metal spring and those which work on compressed air, is much the same.

The first thing to do is to bring your spear back into your hand. If your line is long and you have a reel, you simply work the reel to bring back your spear. If the line connecting your spear with your gun is short, and you have no reel, you bring the spear back simply by pulling in your line. You then insert the spear into the muzzle of your gun and push it down as far as it will go with ease, holding your gun and spear thus inserted in your left hand with the muzzle pointing to the sky. During this time you are treading water with your legs. Your head is sufficiently near the surface of the water and your breathing freedom is unimpaired. This is relatively easy as your fins provide a much larger treading surface than your bare soles do. But it does not matter if you slowly sink while doing this. Come back slowly for air.

The next thing to do is to detach your loader from the belt of your trunks and take it into your right hand. Place the loader on top of the spear. Continue to grip the barrel of your gun with your left hand as near the muzzle as possible. Grip the rest of the gun with your legs in whatever manner you find most convenient, following generally the same principles which you would follow if you were climbing a rope and place the top of your foot below the trigger handle. With a short gun place the trigger handle above your knee.

Just before you have begun to do this, take a deep breath, because the moment you have put your legs around your gun and are gripping the gun with your left hand and your right hand is holding the loader, you are left with nothing with which to swim. You will therefore begin sinking slowly. Never mind! You will not go down very far in the second or two. Push your spear down by exerting pressure on the loader with the index and third fingers of your right hand as hard as you possibly can until you hear the click indicating that the spear is well in and that your gun is cocked.

I have given two illustrations of the positions you are likely to find yourself in, but every fisherman has a different way of gripping the gun with his legs, and upon that will depend his position.

Be careful that the tip of the spear never points to any part of your body. If by chance the spear does escape from your hand you must be careful to prevent its hitting you.

Before you begin loading see to it that there is no boat near you, that there are no other people bathing near you nor other fishermen fishing near you. If you cannot be alone while loading, never let your gun point at anyone while you load it.

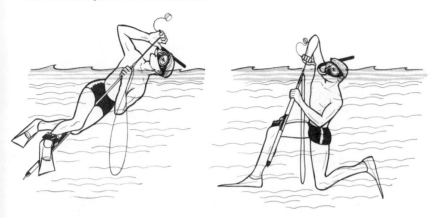

Loading the guns in the water. Left: *Longer guns.* Right: *Short guns*

Loading the gun on land is, of course, far easier. In fact, it is so easy that you may use too much force and you may bend your spear or even break your gun. There are two ways of loading on land:

(a) By resting the point of the spear against a towel, a piece of wood or something soft on the ground, and pushing the gun down on to it. In this position care must be taken not to bend the spear or damage its point.

(b) As in the water, but with the butt of the gun resting on the ground. The danger of this position is that the spear may escape and injure somebody, or at the very least break your line.

One thing to remember is never to walk about on land with your gun loaded. There is no safety-catch system on any of the guns that I have seen which is comparable to the safety-catch systems on revolvers, rifles and guns—and even those, we all know, should not be carried loaded.

GENERAL REMARKS

You should, at the beginning, try to avoid excessive diving or merely going too often under water and holding your breath. The effort of going down to a depth of about five or six metres spending a few seconds under water and coming up again is great. The strain is considerable. The human body will in fact easily withstand the change of pressure experienced at these depths but even then one should avoid straining one's system too much.

The beginner should therefore avoid trying to go to greater depths than six metres and he should be satisfied with the kind of fish he will find in shallow waters.

It is useful at the beginning to take frequent rests at the surface of the water in between your dives. If you have not got a friend with a boat nearby, the most useful thing to have near you is a lifebelt or perhaps the inner tube of a motor-car type, which you might anchor by means of a line and a stone or drag with you all the time. You can rest your gun on it, and by holding on with one hand you can relax for a few minutes. In California many spearfishermen go out with a surfboard. I am not an experienced user of surfboards so that I would find this very difficult and in any case your speared fish and anything else you have on the surfboard may slip off.

LEAVING THE WATER

When you have had enough, swim back to the place where you have left your towel and your spare trunks and the rest of the gear you have not taken into the water.

Before you are ready to leave the water you must discharge your gun. If you are accompanied by a boat, press the tip of the spear against a solid part of the outside of the boat and pull the trigger, gradually releasing the pressure. Be careful that nobody is directly behind you as you may not be strong enough to prevent the gun recoiling hard. The same method of discharging your gun applies to releasing the spear against a rock. If none is handy, place your loader in the loading position and reverse the loading operation by pulling the trigger with the left hand and gradually releasing the pressure of the right hand on the spear. Your line may break if you fire into the open sea space around you. If the water is deep or dirty, you may lose your spear.

The greatest problem, even for the most experienced spearfisherman, is coming out on a rocky shore when the waves are strong. I shall describe a way of getting out which ensures the greatest safety in such circumstances.

If there are no waves, so much the better, but it will do no harm to follow the rules which apply in the case of waves. Swim towards

The special stern opening on the author's diving launch, 'Taro', enables the diver wearing fins and Aqualung to enter the water easily under any conditions and return. Photographs: John I. Thorneycroft & Co. Ltd

the rocky shore, watching the movements of the waves constantly. Keep dipping your head under water from moment to moment so that you can see what is below you. You will now realize the importance of having chosen a good place to begin with. Try to see if you can find a place that affords even a little protection from the oncoming waves. Try to reach out and place, or if necessary, throw your gun and the spear on the rocks so that they will not slip down again into the sea. Do the same with your fins as you will be very clumsy with fins everywhere except when actually swimming. Grab the rocks with your hands. Only when you have managed to clamber out beyond the danger of slipping back and when you can stand safely on your feet, should you take off your mask and find your way to your small camp. In spite of these hints, I should advise beginners to avoid fishing when waves are strong.

If you have to negotiate the breaking waves before you reach shallow water on a sandy or pebbly beach, you have to contend with a strong undertow. You must watch the breakers coming behind you and you must remember that a gun dropped among breakers is difficult to find. The sand or mud or weeds are all churned up and you would have to feel about in this foggy mess for your gun with the waves breaking on top of you.

Let the waves carry you in towards the shore. Keep your head pointing to the shore and your body and legs behind it. Do not let your body go parallel to the waves or you will get rolled over. Let the minimum area possible be exposed to the full force of the waves. Go in the way a boat does and keep your gun close to you along the same axis as your body or it will get wrenched out of your hand. You are always safe from the breakers if you keep your body at right angles to them all the time, i.e. if your head points in the direction in which the waves roll. Continue swimming to avoid touching the bottom. You will thus not step on anything unpleasant in the churned-up water. Rays, sharp stones, broken tins and bottles are some of the hazards.

Only when you are on the shore side of the breakers and cannot swim any more and are like a stranded whale should you stand up and then turn sideways. Go sideways up the steep incline of the last few yards of sand or pebbles in the manner of a skier going up a slope. In this way you will be able to take on your leg and hip the buffeting of what has remained of the waves and the undertow. Then take off your fins and mask and walk out of the water.

5

BREATHING UNDER WATER

Oh, to be a Frog, my lads, and live aloof from care!
THEOCRITUS
Idyl X, 1.52, c. 270 B.C.

OXYGEN APPARATUS AND THE AQUALUNG

The last few years have seen great developments in equipment which enables a diver to spend considerable time below the surface, moving about at ease and being independent of any air-supplying machinery above. We are at least able to spend some time below the surface swimming about like the fishes, moving in a three-dimensional world. We can carry lead weights around our waists to counteract the buoyancy of our bodies and breathing apparatus. Our weightless bodies can thus move up and down, left and right, backwards and forwards. How has this come about? What has made amphibians of us?

We happen to be members of a generation in which breathing under water has become possible. We now have means of taking with us, without any serious impediment to our free movement, what we need to be able to stay under water. A large quantity of oxygen or air come down below with us, stored under great pressure, and we can use it as though we were up in the free air.

There are two principal types of independent breathing apparatus.

OXYGEN

The first type is the oxygen (rebreather or closed-circuit type) apparatus in which pure oxygen is used. The exhaled gas is purified by passing through chemicals which completely remove the carbon dioxide present after exhalation. Fresh oxygen is thus re-admitted as it is consumed in the body. A breathing bag is connected into the circuit to allow for the pulsations of inhalation and exhalation.

Over the centuries the magic figure of six fathoms (twelve metres) has come to indicate the boundary between water more or less accessible to Man and the great mysterious blue depths. Shakespeare prefers the figure of five fathoms for this boundary.

It has been found that oxygen, breathed for any length of time below this depth, is ultimately poisonous to the human body. Thus, while a man equipped with oxygen apparatus may spend an hour or an hour and a half (the normal period for present-day oxygen apparatus) at depths of less than those indicated here, he is sure to be poisoned sooner or later if he makes a habit of going deeper than this, though, of course, he may escape with his life as men have also sometimes escaped from gas-filled rooms.

We must thus definitely place depths below twelve metres out of bounds for the use of oxygen. There are also specific dangers inherent in the oxygen apparatus itself. The absorbent for carbon dioxide is not yet completely reliable and poisoning may result. Caustic solutions may be formed should water accidentally enter the apparatus. Contact of oil or grease with oxygen could cause an explosion.

I hope I have, with these few words, removed the oxygen apparatus from the plans of the beginner. Even though he may wish to keep above a depth of twelve metres he should not use this apparatus before being properly coached. We must leave this apparatus to the military who have uses for it when they wish to engage in operations without tell-tale bubbles appearing on the surface.

THE AQUALUNG

I shall henceforth, for the sake of brevity, refer to this apparatus as the Aqualung*.

Large quantities of compressed air are stored under high pressure (twenty-three hundred pounds per square inch or about one hundred fifty atmospheres) in a unit of one, two, or three steel

---

*I hope the makers of other air-breathing equipment will forgive me if I use the word 'Aqualung' for convenience and in tribute to the pioneer in the same spirit in which other makers of waterproof coats tolerate the 'Mackintosh'.

or aluminium cylinders strapped to a diver's back. This is an open circuit, demand valve apparatus. The air coming out of the cylinder is first dropped in pressure by a reducing valve to a little above that of the surrounding water. A second section of the apparatus, the demand valve, is moved by the negative pressure or relative vacuum created by the inhalation of the diver, thus permitting the passage of low-pressure air fit for breathing. On exhalation, the demand valve is automatically closed and the foul air passes directly into the water. This is an invention of Captain Jacques-Yves Cousteau of the French Navy and Mr Emile Gagnan, and it is generally now known by its American trade name of Aqualung. In Great Britain the famous firm of Siebe Gorman produces it under licence and it is known commercially as the 'Ess-Jee'. There are also German, Italian and Spanish variants of compressed-air equipment, each with its particular points, but all based on the original Cousteau-Gagnan patent. We live in times of rapid development and there are constant improvements.

Captain Cousteau himself has given a graphic and enchanting account of the working of his apparatus in his classic, *The Silent World*.

Let us make one thing plain at the very outset. It has come as a surprise to us how easily the human body can adapt itself to life under water. But we should temper our enthusiasm for the new world by serious reflection. Man, as his body now functions, is not meant to live in a world of water. If he insists on going into the undersea world there are some grave problems he must face, all of which stem from his physiology, and which cannot be solved for him by a machine, however ingenious or efficient.

Before anyone begins to use this apparatus he would be well advised to make quite sure that this important matter is clear to him. Only an expert teacher can explain in detail the problems which I can but mention in a short chapter of a book devoted to all aspects of spearfishing.

Only when the knowledge of the problems involved in going deep below the surface is widespread, will my warning 'Do not play with water' be properly understood.

When I wrote my first book on spearfishing over twenty years ago almost everyone who read it was a beginner. Indeed, it was the first book in English to tell people how to do things in spearfishing (and the first in Serbo-Croat, in its Jugoslav edition that appeared

Ready for action. This posed photograph shows a mini-moke that can reach the shore, a rubber dinghy, camera, Aqualung, and other equipment – and a pair of irrelevant water skis.
Photograph by Roberto Dei

at the same time). There were then no more than two or three books of instruction for beginners in French, Italian or Spanish.

There was then no point in going into the use of the Aqualung, description of the apparatus itself and the dangers involved because there were very few Aqualungs about and even fewer competent teachers.

It may be all very well to try to learn to play golf, football, cricket or baseball or to learn various crafts from 'how to' books. But teaching the use of the Aqualung is for the individual expert teacher and not for the writer of books.

I would not wish to make myself responsible, even in the

remotest or most indirect way, for accidents that might arise through incomplete knowledge or failure to heed warnings of the perils involved.

This was also true of the responsible men who wrote in French, Italian and Spanish at the time I first did.

The real dangers in the use of the Aqualung are made more grave because its use appears to be so simple and easy.

Before you have your first lesson in the use of an Aqualung from a competent and qualified teacher (and not from anyone else who happens to be around and may have used it several times) you must be skilled and practised at getting in and out of the water, swimming and diving with mask and fins in the way I have described these actions in the first four Chapters of this book. Any sudden unsolved problem arising out of these elementary procedures may prove fatal when using the Aqualung. Above all, the elementary ability to swim long distances in circumstances tougher than in a swimming pool must be attained.

By the time my second book came round in 1955, there was much more knowledge about conditions under water, breathing compressed air under water, and there were also qualified teachers.

Even so, I warned in my new Chapters on 'Breathing under Water' and 'The Human Body and Pressure' that the use of the Aqualung was not for the beginner in spearfishing.

Now, as I write again in 1973, I must record a new development. In all of the Mediterranean and almost everywhere else the use of the Aqualung for spearfishing has been banned for the inexperienced man or woman and, of course, for beginners too.

There is, therefore, really no point in writing about the use of the Aqualung for the novice or, for that matter, for anyone whose primary desire is to spear fish under water.

Nevertheless I have revised these two Chapters. Why?

The new discovery Man made (first in the persons of Captain Jacques-Yves Cousteau and Emile Gagnan) of being able to breathe and move in three dimensions under water is so sensational and promising for the future that even a book for beginners under water must give some account of it. With all due warnings, of course, at least an elementary mention is necessary.

That is all that these two amended Chapters do and nothing else.

Where it is still possible, I myself fish with an Aqualung only for big game; sharks and larger groupers and large pelagic fish like barracuda, amberjack and the larger jacks. And I do so near the maximum depths that it is wise to descend to—forty metres off coral reefs, accompanied by experienced friends and never alone, away from other types of fishermen and in places that no other spearfisherman, unless he is equipped with a powerful motor cruiser or a boat with an outboard motor could possibly reach.

The fundamentals for novices at Aqualung diving are taught in different ways but they are constant.

Here is my method.

A. BASIC ASSUMPTIONS

1. You are a generally fit person and you are no younger than 16. We do not know if all parts of the human lung, some of which are most delicate, are in any way seriously affected by pressure differences in the components of air or by excess of carbon dioxide if these lungs are still in the process of growth and development. The same applies to the heart and arteries and veins. Without going too deeply into this subject, I assert that I do not approve of people under sixteen years of age using the Aqualung. I may be erring on the side of caution. My answer to young readers is 'Too bad!' or 'Read another book or go to some other qualified expert and if he lets you do it and something happens, do not blame me.'

2. You are a generally fit person and you are not over forty. If you are over forty and are a really good and experienced swimmer and are generally fit but have simply not had the opportunity to learn, then go ahead. But try not to delay it till you are fifty years old.

3. You can swim at least ten metres under water without mask and fins; climb in and out of swimming pools and can dive down and see and pick up a coin at a depth of three metres, even without a mask.

4. You can do the same with a mask and fins and also put on and take off your mask while swimming or treading water.

5. You can do the same as under 4, but also using a snorkel.

6. When I say a generally fit person, I mean that a landlubber doctor has passed your heart, nose, sinuses, throat, ears and lungs fit. Landlubber doctors are usually ignorant of the problems under water, except in a general way, so they are inclined to be cautious. Quite right. If you pass one of them you are a generally fit person as herein assumed.

If any processes described above, which I am assuming you can perform, cause you any serious nervousness, claustrophobia, hydrophobia (in its original sense of horror of water), not to mention hysterics, please abandon all thought of Aqualung diving. You would be like a novice car driver who cannot stand travelling faster than five kilometres (3 miles) per hour, who cannot stand the smell of petrol or oil, nor can see beyond his outstretched hand even with glasses on.

B. BASIC UNDERSTANDING

1. To be able to deal with the problems that may arise under water is not always a case of presence of mind, stamina or courage. Some of the problems are set by the limitations of the human body. A fine spirit cannot overcome them.

If, for instance, your ears hurt as you go down, and no amount of pinching your nose and pressing air against the nose will alleviate the pain, give up instantly and go up. Gathering all your courage and continuing to go down will only, and inevitably, result in a burst eardrum. It is as simple as that.

2. *Never, but never,* dive with a cold. Your mouth/nose/ear system will only clog up with the excess mucus being driven into your sinuses or your lung. You may damage any of these parts of your body for ever.

C. PROCEDURE IN TEACHING THE USE OF THE AQUALUNG

All qualified teachers will, in one way or another, go through these procedures, having first made certain that the basic assumptions are proved and that the basic understanding exists.
Here is what I recommend:

A. In a swimming pool
1. While standing up to your neck in shallow water, put on your fins.
2. Have someone help you put on your Aqualung and explain to you how the harness and belt work. Take the Aqualung off and then put it on again yourself, still standing in shallow water.
3. Put on your weight belt and ask someone to explain how it can be undone. Undo it and put it on yourself again.
N.B. If the Aqualung harness also incorporates a crutch strap, be sure the weight belt is *above* the harness belt. It is the weight

belt that has to be taken off first in an emergency and, of course, at all other times at the end of a dive.

4. Put on your mask. The snorkel should *at all times*, even when apparently unnecessary, *be fixed* to your mask strap. You will often need it.

5. Put the Aqualung breathing tube in your mouth, whilst your head is still out of the water and breathe in and out several times to see how it feels to breathe only in and out of your mouth. Snort into the mask to see if you can do that.

6. Put your entire head under the water by bending your knees a little and, still standing, repeat what you have just done by following 5 above.

7. Lift your feet gently off the bottom of the swimming pool and bend your knees to see that you are gently sinking. If you are not, you need more weight till you are gently sinking in this position. Stand up, and with your head out of the water take off your weight belt and have someone put another lead weight on it. Replace the belt. Check again.

8. Having satisfied yourself that, as under 7, you are gently sinking, stretch yourself into a horizontal swimming position. Your teacher should be holding your hand all the while and helping you to get into the horizontal position. Your teacher should also have an Aqualung, mask, fins and weight belt on.

9. Swim under water, still holding the teacher's hand. To swim, you need only to move your legs in the crawl stroke from the hips down, not the knees, but the legs and the rest of your body should be relaxed.

10. When you have swum a few lengths, bend your body at the waist and flip your legs upwards and go on moving your legs in the crawl stroke. You should be able to reach the bottom.

11. Swim along the bottom and pick up any coins that have been dropped there for the purpose.

12. Your teacher then attracts your attention and takes his breathing tube out of his mouth, pauses, then puts it back into his mouth and goes on breathing. Do the same several times.

13. Roll over on your back and stay like that for a while.

14. Roll over completely and resume the horizontal swimming position.

15. Go down vertically and pretend you are making a handstand, which should be easy compared with the same feat on land.

16. Sit down on the bottom.

17. Lie down on the bottom.

18. Swim to the shallow part of the swimming pool (where you could, if necessary, stand up with your head out of the water) and sit down. Your teacher will place over your lap a weight belt of, say, five kilogrammes to keep you sitting down quietly and comfortably.

19. Your teacher will then also place a heavy weight belt over his lap and take off his mask, but will keep his Aqualung breathing tube in his mouth and go on breathing to show you that, even with your mask off, you are only myopic with water in your eyes but that, as you continue breathing, all will be well and water will not enter your nose.

Your teacher will then put his mask on again. It will be full of water and he will still be myopic but will go on breathing. He will then hold his mask, one hand on each side, and bend his neck backward until his head is horizontal. He will then snort air from his nose into his mask, gently raising the bottom of the mask. His snorting will emit air from his nose at greater pressure than the water in his mask and push the water out of his mask into the swimming pool. He will then bring his head back and show you what has happened. Some, but not necessarily all, of the water will have gone out of his mask.

He will repeat his snorting with his head horizontal and looking upwards until his mask is cleared of water. There will still be some drops of water on his eyelashes. Capillary action will keep the water there, and if it is sea water this will still smart a little. A few blinks of the eyelids will clear this.

Now do what your teacher did as many times as you think it necessary until you are certain that you can do it.

I always hold my pupils by the waist or legs during this procedure to show them that I am still around while this is going on.

20. Having discarded the heavy weight belt from your lap, watch your teacher go down to the bottom. When he reaches the bottom he will take off his weight belt and place it over one thigh. He will take off his fins and let them float up on their own. He will, still keeping his breathing tube in his mouth, take off his Aqualung and place it on the bottom, shoulder straps up. He will then, keeping his mask on, take his Aqualung breathing tube out of his mouth and gently float up, *whistling air out of his mouth all the*

while. Later in this book you will see why this is necessary. For the moment let me say that air in your lungs when you are below the surface is *compressed* to equal the pressure of the surrounding water on the body. As you go up, the air in your lungs will expand. If you do not let it out as you go up, the expanding air may damage your lungs.

Your teacher will then dive down again and grab his weight belt (which he will see as he still has his mask on). He will then put the Aqualung breathing tube in his mouth and in a relaxed way put his Aqualung on and then place his weight belt around his waist.

Repeat this after him.

Next time, do this having also taken your mask off and left it at the bottom just before letting go of the breathing tube. Your descent this time will be myopic. Never mind, you will see enough. The first thing to do is to put your breathing tube into your mouth and then, to help to keep yourself down and steady, grab your weight belt and put it over your thigh. Then comes the job of putting on your Aqualung while still myopic. Last of all, remember where you left your mask. Even with water in your eyes you should be able to see it. Put your mask on again and clear it of the water as described. Then put your weight belt round your waist.

B. In the sea

1. Go through the entire procedure in section A in shallow sea water.

2. Dive, with your teacher holding your hand, to a depth of six metres, pinching your nose and blowing against your pinched nose to clear your ears. If your ears ache, give up and try another day after you have been in the sun longer in the hope that excess mucus in your nose, sinuses and Eustachian tubes will have dried up a bit.

Repeat the entire procedure under A in deeper water.

If you can never achieve going to this depth without your ears aching, give up the Aqualung.

3. Dive with your teacher to ten metres. Leave everything on the bottom in the sequence you by now know. Your fins will float up but remember to abandon your breathing tube last of all and swim up slowly, at the speed of your bubbles, *whistling air out all the time*. Remember as you go up that the air in your lungs is

expanding and your lungs will continue to feel full. You will, contrary to expectation, not get a message to your brain that you need another breath.

Your teacher, who will keep all his equipment on, should be coming up with you alongside, holding you by the waist to stop you going up too fast and have his own breathing tube ready, if for some reason you panic and desire another breath.

4. Do the same from twenty metres.

5. Do the same from thirty metres.

6. If you are a novice, do not do this from any greater depth. In any case you should *never* go deeper with an Aqualung than forty metres.

7. You should now be ready for your first promenade under water and feel that if anything goes wrong with your mask or Aqualung you can always discard the weight belt and Aqualung and quietly come up.

Learn to breathe slowly but deeply, and move in a relaxed way. This will prevent you using up your cylinder too quickly.

The large single cylinder of the Aqualung will allow an expert to breathe just below the surface for a period of over one hour. As he goes deeper, each one of his lungfuls will take out more of the compressed air from the Aqualung. In other words, he will, as he goes down, breathe in air where the atoms of oxygen and nitrogen are more and more tightly packed. This more tightly compressed air prevents his ribs and lungs from collapsing under the ever-increasing pressure of water on his body. Amazing though it may seem, the body automatically draws just the right quantity necessary all the time and at each depth.

At a depth of ten metres of sea water, where the pressure of water is twice the pressure at the surface, i.e. two atmospheres, the diver will require twice the amount of air to fill his lungs than he would need on the surface. Therefore, at this depth his cylinder will last half an hour. In thirty metres of water his air will last him fifteen minutes. Just to rub the point in—at a pressure of eight atmospheres at about seventy-seven metres, his total time under water will be seven and a half minutes, instead of the hour just below the surface. The air at all these depths will not become toxic and can be breathed freely. The Aqualung and, of course, the other makes of air apparatus based on the same patent are free of the risk of explosion and poisoning. It would be more correct to

Sharks can also be speared. This one was shot from above, on the right side and in the gills. It was a feat for the spearfisherman with an Aqualung to get near enough for a shot.

Photograph by Roberto Dei

say that even air will become doubtful at certain great pressures but we are not concerned with that here.

It will be obvious to the reader that the grave dangers of which I will give but a brief account in Chapter 6 all stem from the construction of our body. They have nothing to do with the efficiency of the Aqualung. We subject our body to certain conditions and only if we act in the prescribed way are we safe. It is not the inventor of the equipment or its manufacturer or seller who are responsible for the creation of these dangers. They lie inherent in the adventure itself and in our bodies.

I do not propose in this book to describe the oxygen or compressed-air apparatus. Each diver will have to know all details of their construction and method of their use so intimately that a mere description in a book cannot be adequate. It is also advisable to agree with fellow divers on hand signs under water to communicate basic information, such as 'come here', 'go up', 'lack of air', 'ear-ache'.

Having pointed out the inadequacies of independent breathing apparatus, let me say that to use one and be able to glide weightlessly in the three-dimensional world under water is an experience which we will have to leave the poets to describe.

It answers one of Man's most ancient dreams—to be able to fly—in a manner so satisfactory that I, for one, am prepared to wait a long time till we can fly like birds.

The equipment is still expensive. This is a relatively rich man's pastime unless clubs are formed and the apparatus is shared. The difficulties of getting one's cylinders filled with compressed air to a pressure of 150 atmospheres (twenty-three hundred pounds per square inch) are prodigious. Oxygen factories, if supplied by the diver with suitable connecting appliances, will do the job of supplying air when not engaged in producing oxygen. It is sometimes possible to have this done at airports too, but individual compressors still cost a great deal of money and need great care and maintenance. Many shops selling Aqualungs provide cylinder-filling as part of their service, for a modest fee.

Finally, I have a summary of a few general rules to give from my own experience of the Aqualung. *They should, however, not be taken as a sufficient guide for prospective divers.*

Have your lungs, heart, ears and sinuses examined from time to time even if you were pronounced fit before you started. Do not dive unless you feel fit. You may cause irreparable damage to your lungs, ears and sinuses if you dive with a cold. If you try and force air through mucus blocking your sinuses or Eustachian tubes, you can easily do lasting damage to tissues. Never dive alone. Also have a friend follow in a boat the bubbles of the air you have exhaled. Do not enter the water in the open sea, keep close to the shore. Time your dive accurately by a wrist-watch. Carry a depth gauge. Do not ascend faster than eight metres per minute and follow decompression instructions carefully if you want, contrary to my advice, to use more than two Aqualung cylinders in twenty-four hours. Be sure that the lead weight belt you wear to achieve balance under water is so strapped around your waist that it can be released in case of need with the speed of a parachute harness. The same applies to the Aqualung harness. Abandon your dive the moment you feel the slightest bit uncomfortable. Check your Aqualung carefully before use and see to it personally each time that it has the full amount of compressed air it is capable of holding. Always wash it in fresh water after use. Rinse the demand valve in fifty per cent alcohol. Do not fill Aqualung cylinders beyond their prescribed pressure. Protect them from sharp blows. Have them tested periodically. In most countries checking is prescribed by law. Keep your breathing tube and demand valve clean and have them re-conditioned at least once a year.

It is important to remember that the full information supplied by the makers of the Aqualung should be known to users. All makers now give some information on the functioning and maintenance of their apparatus. I cannot stress enough that divers should really try to understand the dangers involved in trying to become amphibious.

6

THE HUMAN BODY
AND PRESSURE

Mors sola fatetur quantula sint hominum corpuscula (Death alone discloses how insignificant are the puny bodies of men). JUVENAL
Satires

I suppose that all who have bathed, either in fresh water or in the sea, will remember the first occasion when they put their head under water. The sensation experienced when first putting one's mouth, nose, ears and eyes under water is one which no human being forgets easily. Most of us think it is unnatural to do so and, indeed, most children are inclined to yell their heads off when they are first made to do it. Some of us never again feel like repeating the immersion, and we are sure that the experience we remember was our first.

We are, of course, quite wrong. We have forgotten that each one of us has spent about nine months floating about in a balloon filled with liquid inside our mother's womb, anchored to her by our umbilical cords. We extracted what we needed for life from the liquid surrounding us and through the umbilical cord. We have learned that the overwhelming proportion of the elements that comprise our bodies are the same as the elements that make up sea water. Thus it is not as unnatural as it would seem at first sight that we should now seek to re-enter the sea, whence many consider our ancestors originally came.

Should we go down under the sea in the spirit of the native's return or should we look upon ourselves as explorers of a new world?

It would take me too far, in a book of this kind, to examine the arguments which are put forward to show that at some stage in the history of Earth some remote ancestor of ours, in a shape we would be reluctant to acknowledge any affinity to, had crawled out of the

100

sea and decided to make his habitat in the air. On the other hand, this is not the place to record the developments which have produced the faith that at some stage there was Divine interference in what we are pleased to call evolution. Neither I nor anyone else can escape contemplating the phenomenon of the birth of human conscience, and the fact that, in the absence of further knowledge, this phenomenon apparently sets us apart from other beings.

I therefore avoid the question of the spirit in which we should approach the threshold of the undersea world and content myself with beginning this Chapter with two simple assertions:

Man's body is largely of the same stuff as sea water and Man has spent nine full months of his life totally immersed in liquid.

But even if we start with the advantage of having bodies composed largely of something akin to sea water and with our nine months' experience behind us, there are difficulties to overcome if we seek to become amphibious. I hope to show that we are faced with an adventure which requires much thought before it is undertaken.

In order to survive under the surface, constituted as we are now, we must take down with us air in such condition as will enable our bodies to function so that we can think and move with the same degree of awareness that we possess on land.

It is not enough that the air should just be right for us; we must be able to survive much greater pressure than the pressure of the tons of air bearing down on us when we stand or sit or lie on the surface of Earth.

The invention of the Aqualung which I have discussed in the previous Chapter enables us to stay below the water for periods longer than one natural deep breath can give us.

The use of this apparatus was made possible only by the realization that our bodies, being composed almost entirely of liquid, which is for our practical purposes incompressible by sea water, can stand without any apparent harm pressures far greater than are experienced in an ordinary free dive when holding one's breath.

I shall discuss the problems which arise when breathable air is taken below the water for purposes of breathing. I shall first analyse the effects of pressure on the body and then the effect on the body of air breathed under pressure greater than atmospheric pressure at sea level.

EFFECT OF PRESSURE ON THE BODY

We have established that on diving below the sea and meeting increased pressure by sea water, provided such pressure is applied equally to all the surfaces of the body which is what happens in our type of diving, no harm will be done to us.

We have also found that the anus, the vagina and the canal of the penis can withstand, for our practical purposes, all the pressures the sea water can exert on them.

There remain the inner spaces of the body that contain air and through which air is constantly circulating while we live and breathe. Working downwards, we have the internal and middle ear spaces on the inside of our two eardrums (which themselves provide a seal to the two outer ear canals). Then, by way of the Eustachian tubes, which lead to the mouth and throat, we also have a clear connection to the nose and the four sinuses, the frontal, the ethmoidal, the maxillary and the sphenoid. The canals (ostia) leading to the sinuses are particularly fine and narrow. From the mouth, by way of the throat, the passage of air is led to the lungs. We can call this system the ear/nose/mouth/lung system or, more simply, the inner air spaces of the body.

Provided the pressure of the air in *all* of these inner spaces of the body is equal to the pressure of the surrounding water at any given depth, no harm can befall us.

When Commandant Le Prieur invented the first air-breathing apparatus for use under water (the precursor of the Cousteau-Gagnan Aqualung) he was seized by the problem of these inner air spaces and the effects of increasing pressure of the surrounding sea. He could not risk pressure differences that would destroy the human being. He therefore experimented with a series of valves which would adjust the flow of air from his apparatus at the right pressure for every depth to the mouth and so to these inner air spaces. It was Cousteau and Gagnan who made the sensational discovery that, by the simple action of sucking in air from a cylinder (at a starting pressure of 150 atmospheres) through a reducing valve fixed on the cylinder itself that reduced this pressure through a tiny hole and further, by way of a tube to a demand valve held in the mouth, Man could obtain at all times out of this demand valve, by reflex action and without thinking or further mechanical devices, the right quantity of air sufficient to fill all his inner air spaces including a lungful at *exactly* the pressure of the surrounding water.

Why is this so? This reflex has no practical use to us on land at sea level. (If we went higher and beyond Everest in individual free ascent, the very gradual decrease in atmospheric pressure would involve us in the same process the opposite way.) Yet we have it. I have found no explanation yet to this reflex action except a desire to look further into the nine-month period of our lives bobbing about inside our mother's placenta. Fish have no lungs, but they do have an air bladder, or rather an oxygen bladder, which must, somehow or other, by reflex action achieve pressure inside the bladder equal to the surrounding water. They also therefore have a pressure equalizing system.

We have found that this increased pressure in our inner air spaces has no effect on the heart and the circulatory system. The brain is not crushed under increasing pressure by a collapse of the skull around it because the solids and fluids of the brain and its protective covering occupy the whole space of the 'skull box' and no air at sea-level (atmospheric) pressure can get caught up in it. The pressures inside and outside the skull thus remain equal as the diver goes down. Also the pressure in the flesh of the legs and arms and the rest of the body remains the same as the pressure on these parts of the body of the surrounding water.

If we wore a conventional diver's suit and steel protective headgear, some air would be trapped between the outside water which increases in pressure as the dive proceeds and the body inside the diver's suit and headgear. If, through mechanical failure or other causes, this trapped air were not equal to the pressure of water outside, disaster would occur instantly. If the trapped air were below the pressure of the surrounding water, the body and the head of the diver would be 'squeezed' and crushed and if it were the other way round, a 'blowing up' would take place.

Perhaps to our surprise, we thus find that the naked human body is able to stand changes in pressure as easily as fish can stand them. The naked diver is not so much out of his element under water as he may at first glance have thought he would be.

We can thus say that the greatest practical problem we have are these inner air spaces. Provided the air passages between the lungs, throat, mouth and middle ear spaces and sinuses are clear, the pressure in these air spaces inside the body is constantly equal to the pressure on the body or the outside.

A discussion in detail of this circuit of the inner air spaces of the body is necessary because this is where trouble may occur.

1. Ears and sinuses. My illustrations show the anatomy of the ear and sinuses, which at this stage will help in understanding the analysis of the effects of pressure that follows.

The eardrums completely seal off the outer ear canal from the middle ear and internal ear space. Normally neither water nor air can pass through the eardrums. The middle ear space and the internal ear spaces are connected with nose, sinuses, mouth and throat by canals known as the Eustachian tubes. The throat is, of course, connected with the lungs to complete the circuit.

The only natural openings of this circuit to the outside of the body are therefore the nose and the mouth.

The nose could be tightly closed by a nose clip worn inside the mask. Without a nose clip the nose is open into the mask. The mask contains air and this air space is limited by the closed seal of the mask on the face. By short snorts of air from the nose into the mask, the pressure of air inside the mask is automatically made equal to the pressure in the rest of the inner air circuit.

The other opening, the mouth, is, of course, connected to the Aqualung by holding the demand valve mouthpiece in the mouth with the lips tightly around the neck of the mouthpiece. Air is sucked in and having done its job by filling the lungs, it is expelled again, through holes in the demand valve, into the surrounding waters. It will be remembered that by reflex action the right amount of air for each depth will be sucked in to make the pressure of the inner air spaces equal to the surrounding water.

Let us follow the air through this circuit and see what could go wrong in the ordinary way if pressure of any part of this circuit is not equal to the pressure of the surrounding water.

When air enters the mouth it tends to pass automatically up the Eustachian tubes and into the middle and the internal ear spaces and also into all the sinuses, which are little sacks that spread out from the nasal cavity. If all these passages are free of mucus or an overgrowth of tissue, then the passage of air will not be impeded and all will be well. The pressure of air inside these places will at all times be the same as in the mouth, nose, throat and lungs.

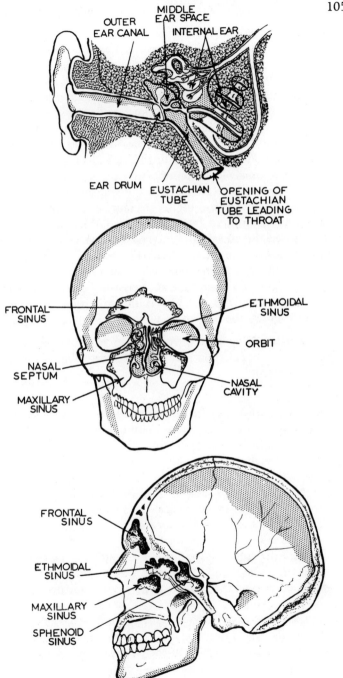

OUTER EAR CANAL

MIDDLE EAR SPACE

INTERNAL EAR

EAR DRUM

EUSTACHIAN TUBE

OPENING OF EUSTACHIAN TUBE LEADING TO THROAT

FRONTAL SINUS

ETHMOIDAL SINUS

ORBIT

NASAL SEPTUM

NASAL CAVITY

MAXILLARY SINUS

FRONTAL SINUS

ETHMOIDAL SINUS

MAXILLARY SINUS

SPHENOID SINUS

If the free passage of air is impeded during a dive, then air at surface and therefore lower pressure, i.e. atmospheric pressure, will be caught in the middle and internal ear spaces, the Eustachian tubes and sinuses and conditions of 'squeeze' will result. Air from the mouth, which will be at higher pressure, i.e. the same higher pressure as in the throat and lungs, will press at the narrow Eustachian tubes and cause intense pain and probably damage to the tissues. Air from the nasal cavity, which is also at the same pressure as the air in the mouth, throat and lungs will also press at the narrow canals (ostia) connecting the nose with the sinuses, and great pain in these passages to the sinuses and damage to the tissues may result. If the higher pressurized air from the lungs, throat, mouth, nose and by way of the Eustachian tubes has not freely reached the middle and internal ear spaces and to the inside surface of the eardrums, then the small amount of air on the outside of the eardrums and in the outer-ear canal (being in direct contact with the water and therefore at increasing pressure) will press the eardrums from the outside. If the difference in pressure is sufficiently great, the eardrums will give way, bursting inwards.

It is worth noting that differences in pressure, even of small degree, will cause pain and may cause damage, even if the eardrum is not perforated.

2. The throat and mouth. These passages are wide enough and strong enough to stand anything the lungs can stand. A frightened diver may cause a spasm to take place in his throat muscles, resulting in a sealing of the main passage from the lung. This could result in the trapping of air in the lungs causing great damage to the lung and perhaps death. The diver should avoid getting frightened or, if he cannot do that, let him not get hysterical.

If a toothache suddenly develops under water it probably means that there is a small gas pocket trapped in the pulp of a decayed tooth where the softer tissue could be 'squeezed' by the increased air pressure in the mouth. The only way to avoid pain is to see a dentist to determine that there are no cavities in the diver's teeth.

3. The nose. If a diver does not suffer from a cold or a deformity in his nostrils, the passage of air through the nose will be easy. This tissue is also stronger than the lung tissues.

4. The lungs

(a) *'Wrong air'*. If the speed of the descent is not more than seventeen metres per minute and if in that minute the diver breathes in and out no less than six times, he will not be caught with the 'wrong air' in his lungs at any moment. By 'wrong air', I mean air at lower pressure being carried inside the lungs to a greater depth where the pressure of water on the body is greater than the air in the lungs. If he descended too fast, the diver's lungs could be 'squeezed' by the surrounding tissue and blood which in turn were being compressed by the water. Constant, regular and frequent breaths and a slow descent ensure safety because the air in the lungs is drawn each time at increased pressure equal to the pressure of the surrounding water.

(b) *Over-expansion of the lungs (Traumatic Air embolism)*. Conversely to the 'squeeze', if a diver begins to rise from a depth and he keeps the air he has inhaled in his lungs, he will suffer a 'blowing up' of his lungs. This 'blowing up' and the degree of damage it will cause to the lungs will depend on the depth from which the diver has begun his ascent and the distance he covered upwards. If he took in a full lungs' breath at thirty-three metres and rose to the surface, the air kept in his lungs will have expanded, as a result of decreasing pressure of the surrounding water as he goes up, to exactly four times the volume. If he kept his mouth closed the air would burst his lungs. I do not need to go into the gory details of the consequences.

To avoid this, a diver must at all times during his ascent avoid a speed greater than eight metres per minute and he must breathe calmly, regularly and frequently, making at least six full inhalations and exhalations every minute. As he approaches the surface, he must reduce his speed to three metres per minute to allow for greater relative changes of water pressure.

(c) *Spontaneous Pneumothorax*. This is an extremely rare phenomenon, even with helmet divers. It can occur with an over-expansion of the lungs. An air pocket may be formed inside the chest cavity but outside the surface of the lungs. As the diver ascends, the trapped air in expanding automatically will collapse the lung and push the heart out of place. I mention it only because it can happen. It will, barring extraordinary circumstances, not occur if the breathing rules explained above are followed both for descent and ascent.

The aptitude of these various passages to let air through varies with each person. Some have no trouble in equalizing air pressures inside these narrow and tender passages in the circuit. I have found that as one becomes more experienced the process of equalizing the pressures and achieving free passage of air through the Eustachian tubes and the ostia becomes easier and smoother. Almost everybody will find some difficulty at first. Ear-ache and pain in the sinus passages are almost universal because the passages are normally never entirely free of mucus. The trick known to airmen of 'blowing the nose' by pinching the nose with thumb and forefinger and blowing air from the lung into the nose, will help in forcing air through the Eustachian tubes. Yawning, if the mouth and teeth can be held tightly over the Aqualung mouth-piece, is the ideal way. Swallowing hard will also help to force equality of pressure into this part of the circuit. As the diver slowly descends he should, by constant repetition of these move-ments, make sure that his passages are clear. He will know if he has failed because he will feel acute pain. He should go up a metre or so and try again. If he cannot go beyond a certain depth he must give up for the day and try again later. If pain persists, it means either that the diver has a slight cold and excessive mucus is preventing the free passage of air, or that an ear, nose and throat specialist should be consulted to discover the reason why he cannot achieve the natural unimpeded passage of air inside the circuit.

Going deeper and creating great pressure on these delicate and narrow channels may do lasting damage and should be avoided. It follows that a diver who has a cold should not attempt to go to any depth at all.

I must add a story about diving with a cold.

I once dived to thirty metres when I had a cold. Somehow I managed to force air through to my middle and internal ear spaces and the sinuses and I felt perfectly well during my dive. As I came out I felt a sharp pain on my right side, somewhere around my lowest front rib. I also imagined that water had entered my left ear. I put the pain on my rib down to the fact that I had rather a tough and difficult re-entry into my fishing boat. The 'water in the ear' had no explanation. Both symptoms persisted.

Upon consulting specialists I found that the 'water in my outer left ear' was in fact accumulated blood, turned into pus, on the *inside* of the eardrum. I had damaged the tissues in the Eustachian tubes and internal ear spaces, fortunately not beyond repair, and my eardrum had to be pierced to extract the pus. It was also found that the 'pain in the rib' was not due to an external blow causing a bruise or a rib fracture. I had forced mucus from my nose down my throat while breathing under pressure. The mucus was forced into the lungs. At the ends of the lungs and around the edges, the bronchial passages get narrower and finer. By blocking these narrow passages with mucus, I prevented new air coming into them from the general stream of air circulation. The congestion produced an infection due to the sudden local predominance of one lot of germs. This process, if I remember the medical aspects correctly, caused a mild state of pleurisy and thus the pain. Fortunately, breathing exercises restored the free passage of air and eliminated the cough I had developed trying to clear my lung of the congestion.

I consider myself very lucky to have escaped with such minor injuries. The story is told to illustrate the folly of diving with a cold, even if one has apparently eased the ear and sinus pain by hard nose blowing.

With the Aqualung, and in spite of greater depths reached, the free diver has an easier task equalizing the pressure inside the air spaces of his body with the surrounding water than a helmeted diver who depends on someone else's judgement and pumping efficiency for the correct amount of air.

The man with an Aqualung can pause every few metres during his descent, blow his nose into his mask and keep on swallowing. He has the time at his disposal to do this at leisure and to make personally sure he has done it, which the helmeted diver does not have.

I must repeat here the injunction against using earplugs. The small pocket of air thus created between the outside of the eardrum and the earplug will remain at surface pressure. When the pressure inside the eardrum and in the outside water increases as the free-diver descends, the eardrum will burst.

THE EFFECT OF BREATHING AIR UNDER PRESSURE

The second group of effects on Man's body when he breathes air under pressure is concerned with disturbances in the equilibrium which surface air possesses for ordinary breathing purposes. Fresh air on the surface is composed of approximately 79 per cent nitrogen, 20.94 per cent oxygen and 0.03 per cent carbon dioxide. There is also a tiny percentage of other gases, for present purposes unimportant. Exhaled air, or air made 'stale' through use in our bodies, is still about 79 per cent nitrogen but about 16 per cent oxygen and 4 per cent carbon dioxide.

There are a few serious 'troubles' which may easily arise. We deal here with the complications that may be caused by nitrogen, oxygen and carbon dioxide under pressure.

1. The effect of nitrogen under pressure. Of the gases making up the air, oxygen, nitrogen and carbon dioxide, only nitrogen will to any appreciable extent dissolve in the blood into liquid form under pressure and after an interval of time. This is a matter of vital importance and every prospective Aqualung user should be absolutely sure that he has not only grasped what I now write but that he has made a proper study of this matter from sources giving much more information than I give here.

The quantity of nitrogen dissolved into liquid form in the blood stream during a dive varies both according to the depth reached and according to the duration of the dive. If, after a long stay at great depth, a diver rises rapidly to the surface, the nitrogen dissolved in the blood will regain gas form all over the body in the shape of separate bubbles, much in the way that bubbles will suddenly be formed if the cork of a champagne or top of a soda water bottle are removed. As the diver rises through water of ever-decreasing pressure, the bubbles will, of course, become larger and may remain lodged in corners in the blood stream, such as elbows, knees and shoulders. The least of the serious results is extreme pain at the affected place as the lodged bubbles enlarge and press on the nearest nerves. Further results may be death or at least lesions on tissues which will have permanent effect depending on where in the blood stream the bubbles had become lodged and enlarged. The limbs and body of a person suffering from the appearance of the enlarged bubbles and their pressure on the nerves will assume the most ghastly contorted positions. Hence the name 'The Bends'. Some people may become permanently bent or paralysed.

It is often forgotten that the two factors—the depth reached and the duration of the stay below—can never be considered separately, and this has caused many fatal errors of judgement in the matter of 'decompression'. Decompression is the name given to the process of getting the nitrogen back into gas form, gradually and all together, by the normal process of the bubbles moving out of the blood stream and being breathed out through the lungs. The Greek coral divers, who have a long and great tradition, dive to depths of over fifty metres holding their breath for a matter of a minute or two. They come up to the surface quickly and in such a case the nitrogen has not had the time to dissolve in appreciable quantities, notwithstanding the depth reached. Even so, these Greek divers sometimes do get 'The Bends' because, though each dive may only have taken a short time, the *aggregate* time under water over any one day may be large.

The world's record for an individual free dive without an Aqualung is now over eighty metres but no man should try and do this more than once in a day.

A long time, i.e. over an hour, with the Aqualung spent in relatively shallow water, will also cause nitrogen to be dissolved in the blood, and even such shallow divers will sooner or later show some signs of having been affected mildly and temporarily by 'The Bends' (Caisson disease).

The Aqualung is so designed that the use of two cylinders in a period of twenty-four hours will not cause 'The Bends'. The deeper one goes, the more quickly is the air used and so the time under water is correspondingly reduced.

All users of the Aqualung should be thoroughly familiar with the 'safety curve' on the Practical Safety graph on page 112 which shows maximum stay at given depths which will make it safe for them to dive without special precautions.

The graph is worked out giving the relation of maximum depth reached to the time spent at such maximum depth, including time of descent and also the time of gradual ascent at not more than eight metres per minute which is good enough for automatic and natural decompression purposes.

Example: If you have to dive to a depth of thirty metres, place a ruler at point A, parallel to the dive duration scale. Where the curve is touched, mark point B. Now place the ruler parallel to the depth scale at point B. Where the dive duration scale is touched is point C, which gives the time of twenty-five minutes. This is the period, including time of descent and ascent, which you may spend

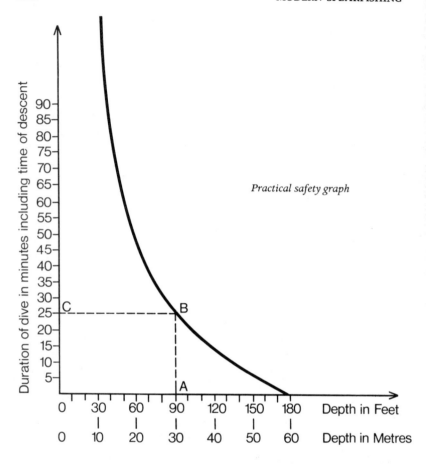

Practical safety graph

at a depth of thirty metres without special care. Twice twenty-five minutes is the maximum aggregate time even if they are made up of several separate dives in one day, if 30 metres are reached.

As this is a book for novice divers I have in this edition eliminated the US Navy standard decompression tables I was, by courtesy of the US Navy, permitted to reproduce in the earlier version. The tables were originally meant for US Navy divers who must, at times, whether helmeted or diving freely, spend much time under water; longer than the equivalent of two Aqualung cylinders in any twenty-four hours.

Anyone interested in diving with an Aqualung longer than twice in any one day should be thoroughly familiar with the decompression tables and also with subsequent studies which show that during the interval up in the air between dives the body automatically tends to bring the liquid nitrogen back into gas form and to eliminate it automatically through normal breathing. Thus, depending on the intervals between dives, it may be safe from 'The Bends' aspect for the expert to dive more often than with two Aqualung cylinders every twenty-four hours.

In the latest Spanish editions of my book these studies and amended decompression data were provided, but here we have entered the field of experienced divers engaged in commercial and other ocean exploration, archaeology, military and naval operations.

2. Cousteau's 'Rapture of the Depths'. This takes place when the diver's body is exposed to air pressures of four atmospheres or more, i.e. at a depth of forty metres or deeper. Oxygen and nitrogen behave differently under pressure and at this depth not enough oxygen reaches the brain cells. There is a decreased ability to work or concentrate and the diver's mood also undergoes a marked change. Mental activity is slowed up and fixations of ideas are apt to develop. A decreased desire to survive may be shown. Errors of the simplest kind creep into any thinking. In many ways, the body reacts as in anoxia (lack of sufficient oxygen) which appears when a person is under alcoholic intoxication (when alcohol in the blood stream burns up oxygen at a fast rate), or at great heights where there simply is not enough of it. The degree of this 'Rapture of the Depths', as Cousteau calls this devil-may-care mood of irresponsibility, varies with different persons. The moment a diver rises to a depth where the pressure is not great enough for this effect to persist, the 'drunkenness' disappears without leaving a hangover. It is thought also that an accumulation of carbon dioxide within the body may be an additional factor for this state.

The only known way of preventing this narcotic effect at greater depths is to mix oxygen with helium instead of nitrogen with which it is normally mixed in the air. Deep dives are now made with a mixture of helium and oxygen, but the helium, for other reasons, can only be added at greater depths. Really deep dives are now made by personnel of several Navies using air or an oxygen/nitrogen mixture of reduced nitrogen content down to certain depths and then switching to an oxygen-helium mixture below. Data on these experiments is not available to the public and is in any case redundant here.

3. Toxic effect of oxygen. I have already discarded the use of pure oxygen breathing apparatus for the beginner, but a reference here is necessary. Oxygen breathed under pressure greater than at about twelve metres deep may produce convulsions which resemble an epileptic attack. Nausea also occurs. The most likely result of the appearance of these symptoms is the loss of consciousness, loss of the mouthpiece and likely consequent drowning. Lieutenant Commander 'Jimmy' Hodges, a former Frogman of the British Navy, lost his life in the Caribbean in 1954, probably from a sudden convulsion of this kind. He was found with his tongue bitten and his mouthpiece hanging on his chest. It is not likely that such an experienced diver had spent too much time below ten metres, even though he had been known at times to dive deeper. It may well be that there was a sudden lack of resistance to the toxic tendency of oxygen at pressure as a result of many months of diving for the expedition he was on.

Normally, at atmospheric pressure, only prolonged exposures to pure oxygen in excess of twenty-four hours will result in signs of irritation. The tragic death of this fine and brave diver has opened an avenue of inquiry regarding the length of time that can elapse before bodily resistance begins to fail when consuming oxygen at greater pressure than on the surface.

Usually, recovery after a minor attack is complete and Dr Hans Hass, whose experience is unrivalled, has managed to avoid any ill effects by staying above ten metres even though his dives have often been of two hours' duration per day.

4. Toxic effect of carbon dioxide. I have mentioned that excess of carbon dioxide may be an additional factor causing the 'Rapture of the Depths'. If carbon dioxide under pressure (and four per cent of the expired air is carbon dioxide) accumulates it may be an additional factor both in 'The Bends' and in the toxicity of oxygen. On its own, carbon dioxide, if more than three per cent of it is present in the air at atmospheric pressure, will cause distress. Under greater pressure the toxic effect, resulting in unconsciousness, is speedier. The only way a diver with air-breathing apparatus like the Aqualung could be in contact with such a critical amount of carbon dioxide is if, for some reason, exhaled air were to accumulate. This is hardly possible in the apparatus as constructed where the 'stale' air (containing four per cent carbon dioxide) that is breathed out is expelled into the water.

It would therefore appear that we can see before us an era in which Man will enter the sea with no greater odds against him than those he faced when he began flying.

The important thing to remember is that we do not know all the factors that come into play when we enter the world of greater pressure. We know some, but there are many still unknown to us. There may be effects of pressure on our bodies which we have not yet detected, and some of us may suffer the direct consequences of our diving without realizing it. We may attribute increasing deafness to heredity, proneness to colds in the winter to our draughty winter homes, and various infections to many causes on land. Yet all of these may be the results of prolonged diving.

The enthusiasm which you develop for spearfishing will dull your judgement on these matters, and you may do yourself harm without realizing it. Do not become a victim of the 'Rapture of the Depths' while you still are on shore.

7

PERILS AND MORALS

A man who is not afraid of the sea will soon be drowned. J. M. SYNGE
The Aran Islands

WEATHER CONDITIONS

It is very difficult to say anything except in the most general terms about the influence of weather on spearfishing. Any details or any advice that one may give concerning one particular region may not be true at all of another place even a few miles away.

There is no doubt that spearfishing is a sport for good weather, at any rate for the beginner. In the Mediterranean this means from about the middle of June until the beginning of the autumn. There will be more fish about in the Mediterranean at the height of the summer and at the time of the oncoming autumn than at the beginning of the summer. There will be many more fish near the shore at times of high tide than at low tide, in spite of the fact that the tide in the Mediterranean is almost insignificant in comparison with those in many other parts of our globe.

Experience has also shown that the first hours of the flow of the tide provide the most fish along the coasts. The prevailing winds and currents in any one region have their effect on the fish in any locality—they will affect the growth of vegetation under water and thus the places where fish may find food. Every point of the coasts of the Mediterranean has its own particular winds and currents and these vary with the times of the year.

Fishing is, of course, ideal when the sea is perfectly calm. In the first place there will hardly be any danger of water entering your snorkel or flooding your mask. If there are strong waves, swimming becomes rather difficult and very tiring. I myself have for years suffered from seasickness in almost any kind of craft. I have been

seasick in small boats, and I have been seasick on the largest
Atlantic liners, but till I started spearfishing I had never been
seasick while swimming in the sea. I must admit that there have
been times when I have been very seasick after about half an hour's
exposure to strong waves. Experience will show that even at
smaller depths the movement of the sea, even when there are
waves on the surface, is quite negligible, and once you are below
you can expect the same conditions under the waves as on a calm
day.

Waves themselves, however, present grave dangers to the
spearfisherman. I have tried in Chapter 4 to describe the ways of
entering and leaving the water in a rough sea. If you are fishing off
a beach, you must make quite certain that you fish fairly far out
beyond the range of the breakers. You run considerable risks if,
when fishing, you get mixed up with the breakers, because you
are not at all equipped for battling with the movements of the
waves with your fins on, your mask on your face, and trying at
the same time to preserve a gun worth a lot of money. You may
get yourself out of breath, and find yourself at the mercy of the
waves. By the time you have gone far enough out off a beach you
will probably find that the sea is too deep, and even there you may
find so much movement of sand that you will not be able to see
very well. If you are a beginner, therefore, you should not fish off
a beach when there are strong waves, unless you are fishing in a
region where you know that there are reefs well beyond the
breakers and there is no other way of reaching them. You may not
feel a current if you have gone beyond a certain depth. Unless you
are very careful and constantly watch the shore, you may find
that you have been carried considerable distances away from the
place where you originally started, and you have not the strength
to go back.

If you are a beginner and the waves are strong, you should also
avoid fishing near a rocky shore. Before you know where you are
you may be dashed against the rocks and hurt really badly, or
knocked unconscious. If you think you are too near shore, dive
and go outwards; it is easier than swimming against the waves on
the surface.

The best times to fish are at dawn and during the last hour or so
of daylight. That is, unfortunately, the time when the water is at
its coldest and your fishing should be of the shortest, but it is

also when the fish are most likely to come to their feeding grounds. If you have discovered those, you will have the best chance of finding fish. You should avoid spearfishing when the sun is at its height and you are most easily visible.

The matter of feeling cold is extremely important. Your body is the best judge of the length of time you should spend fishing. If you feel cold, stop fishing and go out—do not wait to get goose pimples.

Reproduced by permission.
Copyright Punch.

MOTHERS AND WIVES

The first hazard which the new spearfisherman will meet is the objection of his mother to his becoming one at all. If he is married he will find his wife and her mother-in-law united in objecting to this pastime. They find him disappearing from sight for hours on end; they have no idea what he is doing; they resent his escape into another world they know nothing about, and they do not like it. 'No man', said Dr Johnson, 'likes to live under the eye of perpetual disapprobation.' If you cannot find a way of surmounting this hurdle then shut your eyes and ears to Cousteau, Hass and the others and stick to the shore.

FEAR

As I sit in my library and write these words I really feel quite brave about spearfishing. Most of my waking hours on land I feel quite brave about spearfishing. I seldom dream of being under water and I cannot remember a single nightmare in which a pack of sharks were about to tear me to pieces. I have not yet dreamed of being squeezed to a pulp by a two-ton octopus.

I do a lot of daydreaming about spearfishing, not in snatches as Mr Mitty would, but just before going to sleep. Aside from a few delicious moments devoted to savouring imaginary triumphs over sharks and barracuda and landing big groupers, this is the time when fear grips me. I cannot prevent my thoughts from making me dive down between rocks, getting wedged in the deep, bursting with stale air and being unable to break loose. I often think of my line tangled around my feet and somehow anchored to a rock, pinning me ten metres below. I get rolled into unconsciousness by huge breakers. I get cut by poisonous coral and I get cramp in an underwater Rockefeller Plaza, the rocks towering about me on all sides, barring my escape.

I realize that if such events should really occur, it is only fear which would then undo me. I am a good enough swimmer to be able to avoid these disasters and save myself if any of them should happen.

Nonetheless, these fearful warnings should be heeded. The beginner should avoid diving into holes and caves. He should avoid looking into them and poking about inside with hand or gun unless the space behind him and at his side is entirely open. He should have his knife handy and never hesitate to cut his line if he even suspects he might be entangled. Nothing easier than to dive for your spear or gun later with fresh air in your lungs. Cramp is nothing to worry about. If you keep relaxed in all other limbs and do the usual stretching of the affected limb till the cramp grip is released, you will find it easy to swim back to your boat or base. Do not continue fishing if you have had cramp. You are probably out of training or the water is too cold for you. If you are a person liable to have cramp, drink a little sea water from time to time. Anti-cramp salt tablets, made famous by tennis players, are obtainable almost everywhere.

Always try to remember places where you can get out and rest, so that if you are in trouble you will not lose your head just because you cannot see an easy way out of your difficulty in the first moment. When all this is said, the way to avoid fear is to be completely at ease with mask, snorkel and fins even before beginning to fish. Also, the beginner should always be accompanied by a boat.

POISONS AND VENOMS

In 1970, under the sponsorship of the Deputy Chief of Staff for Research and Development of the Department of the US Air Force, the Office of the Surgeon General of the Department of the US Army and the Bureau of Medicine and Surgery of the Department of the US Navy, the United States Government Printing Office published a monumental work entitled *Poisons and Venomous Marine Animals of the World*. The author was Bruce W. Halstead, M.D., Director of the World Life Research Institute and Commander, Medical Corps, United States Naval Reserve. The Sections on Chemistry were prepared by Donovan A. Courville, Ph.D., Department of Biochemistry, School of Medicine, Loma Linda University.

I have before me Volume III—*Vertebrates, continued.*

I have asked to be allowed to say something very briefly about the essence of this large and scholarly volume.

In his introduction Dr Halstead says: 'Venomous fishes constitute a biological hazard to anyone invading their environment. They, like other forms of toxic fishes, offer a rich source of new and little known highly active biochemical agents. Probably less than five per cent of the venomous fish species that are known to exist have been studied even in a cursory manner.' He adds: 'Moreover, the basic chemical structure has never been determined for a single fish venom'. On the particular subject that there is some evidence that the venoms of stingrays, weevers and scorpion fishes (those most likely to be encountered by the beginner—my remark) may be similar or have similar chemical components, Dr Halstead says: 'Our present knowledge is much too meagre to permit one to indulge in generalizations at this time'.

Dr Halstead is no landlubber doctor and so *ab initio* highly suspicious of what he hears of the world under water and distrustful of the legends, hearsay and nonsense which sea-going folk have made their domain.

When *he* says that at the present time little is known, then please accept that little is known.

There are, however, some things he *does* assert. 'The geographical distribution of venomous marine fishes follows somewhat the distributional pattern of fishes in general. Venomous marine fishes are present in greatest numbers in warm temperate and tropical waters. The variety of species decreases as one proceeds in the direction either of cold northern or cold southern latitudes.'

The greatest venom development is found in the family *Scorpaenidae*. There are some of these in the Mediterranean. They inhabit dark caves. Much difficulty of a technical nature has been encountered in classifying the venoms of these and their related stone fishes. They are so well protected by colour and general appearance that one comes suddenly upon them, especially using a torch, almost face to face. So certain are they of the protection of their venomous spines that they are easy shots. They should not be touched or removed from the spear from which they will not try and wriggle off. They are, when cooked after having been cleaned internally, not only safe to eat but constitute the base of every decent fish-extract soup in the Mediterranean from the famous Bouillabaisse of Marseilles down to the poorest Arab broth.

Sea snakes are capable of inflicting fatal bites and some species are aggressive. Anything that looks like a thin snake swimming in the water might as well be avoided. I have been lucky in that after thirty-seven years under water almost everywhere in the world, even the Persian Gulf, I have never even seen one sea snake.

Let me go through the medical aspects of the venoms of fish that I have encountered, making a very brief precis of what Dr Halstead says:

Sharks. Only some sharks possessing dorsal spines are venomous. There are other, fairly serious problems with sharks, so that it is enough to say that you should be careful of sharks with spines. In any event, nothing more than tenderness of the affected part is likely. Encourage mild bleeding of any wound. Antitetanus agents should be administered and the affected part bathed in hot water.

Stingrays. The predominant symptom, which I can confirm from personal experience in Equador in 1955, is pain concentrated around the wound. The pain from a whip of the spine under the tail usually attains its maximum intensity in ninety minutes. It is sharp, shooting, spasmodic and throbbing in character. Stingray venom first of all produces a general shock. It tends to produce vascoconstriction affecting the heart and sinuses. Then it depresses breathing. All or any of these may ultimately cause death. The wound should be quickly cleaned and an attempt made to suck out the poison immediately. Hot water should be applied and a tourniquet if possible. My own severe pain simply ceased completely and suddenly after about ninety minutes. Dr Patrick J. Mullaney, in an issue of the *Skin Diver*, recommends thirty miligrammes of pentazocine lactate intravenously and the same dose intramuscularly to relieve pain immediately. In addition, the area of the wound is infiltrated with two per cent lidocaine as a local anaesthetic.

Weeverfishes have poisonous spines on the back. They can produce violent pain in thirty minutes. They seldom cause death and ultimately, in most cases, the swelling and tenderness subside. Treatment as with stingrays. Intravenous calcium gluconate has been shown to be effective. The diver (who can see under water) is in less danger of stepping on a weeverfish than an ordinary bather, as these when disturbed stay still on the bottom.

Scorpionfishes have been mentioned. The pain can be severe and the general effects of being stung by the dorsal spine are swelling, sometimes constriction of the chest, respiratory distress, convulsions and even death. Treatment is the same as in stingrays, the sooner the better, especially with the related stonefishes. I have found that injections of ·1 to ·5 ml of ·5 per cent (in distilled water) of potassium permanganate was effective. I believe, though I cannot prove it, nor would I dare assert it as a generality, that these potassium permanganate injections in or near the wound are effective very soon in stingray and weeverfish wounds also. All this applies to toadfishes too.

Surgeonfishes produce puncture wounds or cuts by the caudal spines on each side just in front of the tail. The effect is minor. I suggest cleaning the wound, sucking out very soon what there may be of the venom and bathing in very hot water.

Morays (this includes conger eels). Their reputation over the centuries has been tremendous. Dr Halstead has found nothing conclusive but allows that there may be some venom of some kind in the palates of morays. Their bite is not clean and regular and I can see other subsidiary infections following a failure to clean the wound and remove irregularities caused on the skin and flesh by the bite. I have been bitten by several morays with absolutely no ill effect.

There remain the harmless looking blobs of jelly that float about, sometimes in enormous numbers. When they come into contact with the human body they sting. Some people feel this more than others. Obviously the eyes, mouth and other parts of the body where mucous membrane is exposed, are more tender than our skin. Sand rubbed over the infected part or calamine lotion soon soothe the irritation. The Portuguese Man-of-War is a larger jelly with very long (sometimes five metres) and very thin cellular strands. In Hawaii, I once came into contact with a large mass of them as I came up to the surface from a dive. I had a very sharp stinging sensation all over my back as though I had been hit by a very thin whip. On inspection I found that my skin had been lightly lacerated in long lines as though I had indeed received many strokes of a very thin whip.

In all cases the primitive treatment I have described in the various cases mentioned will do until a doctor is found ashore which is something that should be done with all speed, giving the doctor a coherent description of the cause of the accident.

Apart from the problem of a wound on the body through which venom has entered there is also the problem of toxicity; i.e. the poisonous effect resulting from eating fish.

Almost all other fish have been reported as being poisonous to eat somewhere or other. Perhaps this varies according to season and according to the food they happen to eat in any one area. Perhaps the mucus on their bodies, perhaps some glands under the skin, perhaps other causes, have resulted in humans being poisoned after eating fish. Probably this varies with individuals.

Here, turtle poisoning constitutes one of the more violent forms of what the experts call marine biotoxications. Cases have been reported in India of several hundred people dying of turtle flesh poisoning.

At all events, however, ludicrous as it may seem, I have followed local legends and have avoided eating turtles or fish that in any one place the local population considered poisonous. I have probably deprived myself of many a good lunch or dinner, but, then, here I still am.

PASSING CRAFT

Another danger which you are likely to meet is passing craft. As you go swimming about with your eyes pointing downwards towards the sea bottom in quest of your fish, you are not likely to notice anything on the surface. I have found myself hitting my head against buoys and rafts and once a motorboat nearly went over me. When there is a moderate sea, it is particularly difficult for anyone driving a motorboat or rowing a boat to see you. Most of the time only part of your head and the snorkel are visible, and when you are below the water you are, of course, completely invisible to people on the surface. In any case, it is not much use fishing where there are other people about and particularly where there are motorboats about, because fish are very frightened of them and will disappear into the deep water beyond your reach.

INJURIES

The most common injury is grazing oneself against rocks or coral reefs. These injuries should be treated in the same way as any cuts or abrasions. Some people may at first be particularly sensitive to coral burns. I have found that over the years I seem to have developed an immunity to them.

PROFESSIONAL FISHERMEN

One very important word is necessary on the relations of amateur spearfishermen with professional fishermen. Along most of the coasts where you are likely to find fine places for your spearfishing you will be interfering with the activities of the local fishermen. Generally speaking, the view among those who know about spearfishing is that you kill so few fish that you are not doing the fishermen any harm. It is, nevertheless, advisable to make quite sure that you are not injuring anybody's rights, and even if you receive the green light, to keep as far away from professional fishermen as possible.

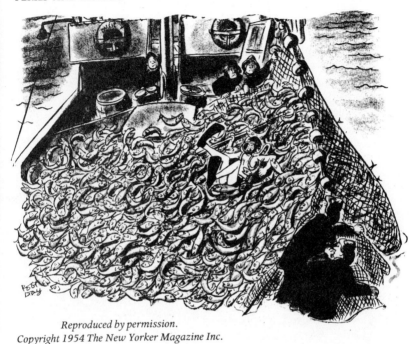

To begin with, you may be a guest in their country, and secondly, you are interfering with an activity which is their bread and butter and which for you is merely a sport. Your presence may frighten away some large school of fish; you may get mixed up with nets and you may generally turn out to be quite a nuisance.

Even so I must elaborate a little on the question of professional fishermen in their relations with spearfishermen. From later sections in this Chapter under the headings 'Voluntary Restraint' and 'Restrictions on Spearfishing', the reader will see that I am not an advocate of wholesale murder under water. Indeed, I am as concerned as the next man in trying to preserve the flora and fauna on land and under the sea.

But our activities simply cannot be compared with the onslaught on whales that has almost eliminated them from the seas. The scientific methods now used in cod, herring and anchovy fishing where the fish are found by underwater sounding devices and are, to all intents and purposes, sucked in on board in their millions every day, year after year, have depleted the oceans in a way quite unimaginable to the spearfisherman who stalks one individual fish at a time. The dragging of the bottom by nets for bottom-dwelling fish, shrimp and lobsters accounts for more depletion every week than all spearfishermen together have done since the mask was invented. To this I add the unspeakable practice of fishing by throwing hand grenades into the sea.

The pollution of the seas by oil, chemicals, plastic articles, etc., is a far greater outrage than all or any of us has committed.

The only divers who have done any real damage are those who professionally dive for lobsters. They, however, belong to professional fishermen and not among we sporting fishermen.

AMATEUR ANGLERS

Alas! they too have become our enemies. In many places spearfishermen have swallowed their pride and self-esteem through their desire to return with some fish, any fish. Having discovered a rock inhabited by, say, groupers, snappers or sea breams, they have polished off the whole place or, worse still, left speared fish lying about injured and dying. This has, at least temporarily, driven other fish away. Some fish really are sitting targets; only cads, for instance, will spear angelfish.

In America, Italy, Europe and some other places, the great growth of spearfishing clubs has given rise to competitions and championships.

None of these activities has helped to assuage the anger of the man sitting outside, dry and relatively comfortable, who has to wait for what comes along and who finds the conditions he knows so well to have become disturbed. His art consists of dealing with a fish that has been attracted to him, while the spearfisherman has the advantage that he stalks the fish of his choice. The difference between us is a matter of taste.

VOLUNTARY RESTRAINT

We cannot dispute with each other in matters of taste. Spearfishermen must remember that they are newcomers and that their responsibilities are greater the more efficient their weapons are. Motorists have only been on the roads for sixty years. They cannot expect to enjoy the ancient rights of the pedestrian. We should establish our own code of behaviour lest we be driven out of the waters along civilized shores by the concerted action of angry anglers. Already in Bermuda you cannot use anything else but a handspear and, as I have mentioned, in many places you must not carry a gun if you dive with an Aqualung.

The range of underwater fauna, even if not so wide as of the animals on land, is great enough to allow for all tastes. You would not chase butterflies with a DDT gun, nor, if you were English, would you shoot a fox. You would not use a rifle for a pheasant or a bazooka for a lion. Each man should make up his mind and go for the type of spearfishing suitable to his taste and ability. Wholesale slaughter and the killing of fish purely for the sake of killing are activities which I should not like to be caught defending. There must be an element of risk or skill to compensate, or at least to try to compensate, for the destruction of life.

A roughly worked out suggestion, allowing for these considerations, is given here as a basis for a scheme of voluntary restraint. The essence of this proposal is that a man should try to fish in a manner which he thinks is just a little too difficult for him:

CLASS A. Beginners of all ages, boys and girls up to fourteen, and spearfishermen of any ability over fifty years of age.

The Hawaiian sling and handspear; maximum depth five metres; fish up to two kilogrammes (four pounds). Only fish intended to be eaten to be speared. No angelfish, boxfish or Californian Garibaldi ever.

CLASS B. Average spearfishermen of ages between fourteen and fifty.

Rubber sling, spring or compressed-air gun, but only for fish beyond five kilogrammes.

A Hawaiian sling and handspear for smaller fish. Only fish intended to be eaten to be speared. No angelfish, boxfish or Californian Garibaldi ever.

Octopus to be caught by hand, no rays, only one lobster or crayfish to be caught by hand each outing.

No fish less than five kilogrammes to be shot at if using an Aqualung where this is allowed.

No fish to be speared at the surface at all. Dives beyond five metres, but not deeper than ten metres.

CLASS C. The experienced spearfisherman should consider himself to be the big-game hunter of the sea.

Powerheads to be used only for large sharks and for scientific
purposes.

No fish to be speared with any weapon at less than six metres'
depth, except with Hawaiian sling or handspear. Spearfishing with
an Aqualung, where allowed, to be restricted to fish over twenty-
five kilogrammes. Hawaiian slings and handspears only to be used
for the less mobile fish under rocks, whatever their size.

Only fish intended to be eaten to be speared, except sharks,
barracuda, morays and also rays not smaller than twenty-five
kilogrammes.

No small fish and those relatively easy to shoot to be hunted
at all.

I am glad to say that since I first postulated these voluntary
restrictions, things have begun to develop along those lines. All
prospective spearfishermen should know the recommendations
issued from time to time by their National Underwater Spearfishing Associations and similar bodies in each country.

RESTRICTIONS ON SPEARFISHING

By now in all of the Mediterranean and in many other places, the
professional fishermen have prevailed on the authorities to control
spearfishing. Spearfishermen must now possess fishing licences
which may be obtained from the local authorities directly or
through membership of spearfishing clubs. So far as it goes, I
think this is perfectly reasonable. The weapons now used are as
dangerous, or almost as dangerous, as some of the land weapons.
I know of one case in the British Virgin Islands where one man
killed another with an underwater fishing gun during a quarrel
in a garage. It makes sense, therefore, for authorities to seek to
exercise some control over the people likely to use these weapons.
In this sense, of controlling weapons, nobody, in my view, has
gone far enough. But, as long as many, even civilized countries
are so very lax in controlling the use, licensing and sale of weapons
on land, we cannot hope to have more care exercised over weapons
for use under water.

Spearfishing with Aqualungs is forbidden on any terms in many
places in response to appeals by professional fishermen.

You can probably get information about obtaining a licence at your hotel or boarding house, or at the offices of the local authorities. The fee for a licence which will take you through the season is usually small.

Some comments from an old hand never consumed by passion may not be out of place.

It will, I hope, have been conceded that the quantity of fish a spearfisherman can land using a spear (mechanical or hand-propelled) is rather small when compared with the results of trap fishing, net fishing or fishing with hooks left on lines anchored overnight, and of course compared with commercial fishing activities anywhere. It cannot therefore be the mere quantity of fish speared that is objectionable in our case.

It is natural for a spearfisherman to try to spear the largest specimen he can find. Human vanity is a sufficient guarantee that most of us will be consistent in this behaviour. Spearing larger fish is where the element of destruction to the breeding stock is brought in.

Before Man appeared, says Professor J. L. B. Smith, it may be accepted that the number of marine fishes in any one area had reached stability. Birds have been present long enough and are familiar enough to us to be considered one of the original factors in the existing 'Balance of Nature'. Professor Smith dismisses the popular conception that it is harmful to this Balance of Nature for men to kill immature fishes. On an average, a fish produces about one hundred thousand eggs per season, only one or two of which, under normal conditions, can reach maturity unless that species is to increase greatly and by so doing upset the Balance of Nature on its own. It is, therefore, much more harmful to kill an adult fish than dozens and dozens of small ones.

I have said what I think of the wholesale destruction of the famous cold water fishes, the cod, herring and anchovy. Shore netters and trappers mainly catch half-grown and non-adult fishes, while spearfishermen can be expected to catch the adults. It is the destruction of adult fish that poses the problem in restriction. Careful study of the consequences of spearfishing in different parts of the world has not brought us to any valid conclusions as to his effective powers of destruction.

There is no question that certain areas at times give the appearance of being 'fished out'. It is common experience, however, that in spots inaccessible to others near these fished out areas, the spearfisherman may still find fish in plenty. Fish learn very quickly and we all know that new methods, new baits or different tackle yield surprising results in areas supposedly fished out. An area may merely only contain wary fishes. After years of spearfishing in some places in the Mediterranean I find, for instance, that I see just as many fine groupers as before but I encounter increasing difficulty in spearing one.

It may, I think, be safe to say that adult fishes who have survived one attack by a spearfisherman will have learned the lesson of their lives. To what extent fish consciously communicate messages and warnings to each other we do not know, of course, but I can tell in an instant when I come upon a settlement of fish whether or not they know what I am. Sometimes an alarm is sounded before I have taken a shot, and it is then that only skill bred by experience and coupled with luck will enable me to spear one.

After a certain period, the fish in any one area should adjust themselves to men fishing under water just as they have coped with other methods of fishing by Man.

If it is still thought wise to restrict spearfishermen's attack on larger adult fish (notwithstanding the scant available knowledge and the likelihood that the fish know best how to protect themselves), how is one to do it fairly?

To ban spring, rubber-propelled guns or compressed-air guns altogether would largely eliminate the peril to adult fish arising out of spearfishing, but it would still leave the field clear to anglers of all sorts. Without getting involved in an argument on the relative efficacy of angling and spearing large fish, I assert that, on present evidence, the elimination only of spearfishing would be unfair to the spearfisherman. One should not forget that there is a considerable element of sporting risk and danger in a man diving seventeen metres or more and meeting large fish in their element, a factor not present in angling.

To ban the use of Aqualungs for spearfishing is, however, a practical measure worth discussing. Nobody going deep with such apparatus would bother with small fish. It is no fun going up and down, allowing for decompression time, etc., just to bring back a small parrot fish, a smaller snapper or a sea bream on each trip. The spearfisherman with an Aqualung will tend to go for one single but larger fish on each dive. This means that if he is lucky, a spearfisherman would bring back an adult fish on each of his two daily dives, since for the sake of his own health he would not make more than two dives daily.

It should be worth considering not totally banning but limiting the use of the Aqualung to outer reefs and areas away from beaches, towns or settlements. This would reduce the number of enthusiasts as it is more costly in time and money to go far. Another measure which might be taken simultaneously, and which is possible on islands, would be to prohibit the import of Aqualungs by visitors but to allow a limited number to be available for hire, the scheme operating under a local organization such as a club.

So, except in the case of the Aqualung, it would seem that measures to restrict spearfishing would be discriminatory to the spearfisherman without removing the evils one seeks to eliminate. There are, however, two considerations which we spearfishermen must bear in mind before crying out 'Unfair'. We cannot complain unless:

All practices which interfere with professional fishermen in any area where fishing is a genuine economic factor are avoided. All practices which interfere with bathers are avoided. I, who object to dogs running all over me when I sunbathe, and to litter strewn all over a beach, cannot be offended if I get chased off a place when I appear spear or gun in hand.

It is up to each spearfisherman individually to exercise that amount of restraint which will allow him to fit into the life of his community or the places he visits without infringing upon ancient rights and customs.

CLUBS AND COMPETITIONS

There are many clubs now in different parts of the world and I hope that their influence will be in the direction of restraint. In Nervi, Italy, there has been for years a spearfishermen's school whose activities were inspired by Duilio Marcante, one of the famous Italian spearfishermen. The Italians were the first to form clubs. In France there are, in some localities, men who are willing to serve as submarine guides. The American magazine *Skin Diver* is full of information about clubs and organized spearfishing tours. Everywhere there are clubs where advice will enthusiastically be given to visiting *aficionados*.

I am fascinated by the names of the California and Florida spearfishing clubs that have come to my notice. The famous 'Bottom Scratchers' I have already mentioned. Some other names are: Reef Rogues, Snorkels, Sharks, Carpinteria Hell Divers, Sea Knights, Kelptomaniacs, Sub-Mariners, Sea Combers, Kelp Kings, Santa Barbara Seals, Water Bugs, Kelp Worms, Davey Jones Raiders, Sea Urchins, Sons of the Beaches, Sarasota Sand Sharks.

In Florida, the Florida Skin Divers' Association appears to be the central body for the various clubs formed, and in California it is the Council of Diving Clubs. In the UK the Sub-Aqua Club of Great Britain has long ago made its appearance.

I feel that the introduction of competitions, or 'Spearfishing Championships' is to be lamented. My lament has not been heeded, but I feel, as the author of a book which may persuade people to take up this new sport, that I have some responsibility. When racing on land and in the water, jumping or throwing, one man may pit his natural gifts or acquired skill against those of another under conditions which are equal for both. In individual or team games, such as tennis, golf or football, equal conditions for both sides exist and competition is natural. In hunting, shooting and fishing this element of equal conditions is not present (except in target shooting and clay-pigeon shooting) and competition in these sports seems to me to be meaningless.

It is sensible, perhaps, to institute rules for local, national or world records in the size of each species of fish speared under some kind of agreed conditions for weapons, and hope that these will be observed. To go further and hold competitions for size or quantity of fish or game killed in ever varying circumstances seems to me to be foolish. One man's superiority over another cannot be proved and the object of the exercise is thus frustrated at the outset.

Such activities must lead to the degeneration of our sport into senseless, wholesale killing. We must avoid paid 'beaters', and exhibiting stuffed sharks in our game rooms killed under conditions similar to those in which distinguished strangers in India were once enabled to kill tigers. Let us, at least, try to avoid making ourselves ridiculous in the eyes of hunters and anglers who have for generations, albeit with some deplorable exceptions, avoided impossible competitions.

UNDERWATER PHOTOGRAPHY

As I have said this is a subject which has merited many books of its own, and I shall not deal with it here.

Dimitri Rebikoff, a Frenchman of Russian origin, is the pioneer of effective underwater photography which has developed greatly since the early days. His book *L'Exploration Sous-Marine*, Arthaud, Paris 1952, has remained a classic. Those interested should seek information from the various magazines devoted to the world under water. I mention some books and two of the best magazines in Chapter 3. The very fact that these magazines have published thousands of magnificent photographs of underwater scenes, both in colour and black and white, is evidence enough that they must be the source of the best and latest information.

FROGMEN

I have already mentioned the frogmen of the last War. By becoming proficient at spearfishing you will have achieved a standard of mobility under water and efficiency at swimming which may qualify you in some future emergency to serve your country in the capacity of a frogman. This is an extremely dangerous occupation, and the technique which is necessary in its pursuit is still relatively in its infancy. It does not take much imagination to foresee a tremendous development in the military usefulness of the frogman.

MANNERS AND FORM

As far as Man is concerned the world under the sea is an entirely new one. So let us look around, as we do when we are strangers in a known part of our world, to learn what local manners are. 'When in Rome, do as the Romans' has been a very useful precept for at least two thousand years.

Under water, the world seems to me like the primaeval jungle, the rain forests or the great deserts. 'The law of the jungle' is a phrase much used, but it is used quite wrongly nowadays to describe the cut-and-thrust of the rougher forces of urban civilizations. But in urban communities so much junk is left after the cut-and-thrust. Not so in the jungle; not so under the sea. All is tidiness in both places. Nothing is left to survive and pollute after the myriad battles for life and death. As a last resort there will be bugs and worms to eat things up and maintain the so-called ecological balance. All organic matter, however it has been left lying about at the end of some battle in the balance of nature, is dealt with satisfactorily and the jungle, the rain forests, the deserts and the undersea world are all left tidy.

The moment Man entered these areas he left a mess.

Under the sea, I have no objection in principle if I find half an orange, Kleenex, egg shells, bread or other food. In the end I cannot object to normal urban drainage and or any other food refuse. Even sardine tins will ultimately rot away and minute particles take their place. Ultimately, glass bottles will break up into small fragments, get rounded off by the friction against stone and sand and finally join the sand in minute particles. But what about fuel oil dregs; what about plastic bottles and sheets, plastic slippers, bags? So far as the life of each individual human being is concerned, these things will survive him, finally polluting some beach, having in the meantime entirely spoilt the free and clean world under water.

Please do not throw into the sea anything which is not organic and which will not disintegrate beyond recognition after a few hours at most.

On board a boat devoted to spearfishing please be tidy about your equipment. Keep it in one place and do not let it get mixed up with anyone else's. Time, at least, is lost in sorting out fins, masks, weight belts, Aqualung breathing tubes, torches, wet suits and so on.

Never, but never, leave a mask where someone might step on it. On my own boat there is never any glass of any kind on board. The only breakable item is the mask and I do not allow that to be left where someone can step on it.

SEA FRONTIERS

The International Oceanographic Foundation, 10 Rickenbacker Causeway, Virginia Key, Miami, Florida 33149 is one of the most civilized enterprises on Earth. Amongst its many activities it publishes a review called *Sea Frontiers* which presents even to the layman many aspects of the world under water. Always highly scientific, in the best sense of the word, it is at the same time

A Blackfin Grouper speared by the author off Andros Island, Bahamas.
Photograph by Eric Weinmann

readable and intelligible to the unseasoned reader.

NEW CAREERS

The mobility which you can achieve under water in using the equipment mentioned in this book is, of course, far superior to the mobility which the helmeted diver can achieve. The inspection of ships' bottoms is now very often carried out by men using the equipment described in this book. In the same manner, inspections of the sea bed or the region near shore may be made for the purpose of engineering and building, or for the study of underwater flora and fauna. The women pearl divers of Japan have found masks essential in the pursuit of their profession. The development of underwater photography has already been mentioned, and many of those who now go under the water with the equipment described do not go to spear fish but to photograph or study fish life, pursue archaeology or make scientific experiments.

There is a wide range of useful jobs that may be carried out under the water now that we have achieved both mobility and the capacity to see below the surface. Many people now cannot even imagine bathing in the sea without having a mask handy in order to be able to observe the world under water.

A simple mask and a pair of fins have wrought a revolution and have helped thousands of people to find an entirely new and different world, a world accessible to almost everybody. Who knows what we may yet discover under the water? We may discover new mines, we may discover new oil wells, we may find lost treasures. We are sure to come across species of fish hitherto unknown. We are bound to make new discoveries among the flora and fauna under sea. We shall learn much. I suppose people have already examined the effects of the atomic bomb under the sea. We may even finally solve the problem of the sea serpent, the mermaid and other monsters of old, even if we do not succeed in spearing them. The mystery of the Loch Ness monster may soon be probed by one of our ilk.

LAST WORD

Spearfishing is a new sport. It involves delving into the unknown. Our generation may consider itself lucky to have had the first

A coral reef.
Photograph by Roberto Dei

chance of combining a new pastime with the adventure of exploring the sea, which occupies over seventy per cent of the Earth's surface.

To probe the mysteries of this unknown but major part of the globe and at the same time to pit his skill, endurance and courage against some of its brave inhabitants is an adventure worthy of Man's finest traditions.

At all events there is much fun to be had. I hope the readers of this book will have some of it.

8

SOMETHING ABOUT FISHES

*No human being, however great or powerful, was
ever so free as a fish.* JOHN RUSKIN
The Two Paths

The great expanses of the oceans are not as full of fish as are the
areas of shallow water near land. This is due to the fact that the
smaller fishes largely depend on immobile forms of life for food.
Light does not penetrate very much below thirty fathoms so that
most fish food grows and flourishes in water less than thirty
fathoms deep. The small fishes eat seaweed, molluscs, shrimps and
bits of coral; bigger fishes eat the little fishes; and the larger ones
eat these. The fish that keep close to the shore are called littoral
fishes. In this book I am concerned with littoral fishes and only a
few of the oceanic or pelagic fishes that visit shallow waters
occasionally for food.

The first list I give is the Mediterranean list. Most of the fishes
listed and briefly described have close cousins in other areas. In
deciding to pick the Mediterranean, I had two considerations in
mind. Spearfishing was born there, and so, to a large extent, was
the study of fishes. It is also a place where many languages are
spoken in a relatively small area, and some part of it is likely to be
visited sooner or later by the British or American enthusiast. This
has given me the opportunity of giving the principal names of the
fishes listed in English, French, Italian, Spanish and Portuguese.

Where I found no English name that fitted my typical example
of the Mediterranean variety I have played safe by giving the
scientific (usually Latin, sometimes Greek, sometimes combined)
name. The scientific name of each genus and family (explained
below) is given in each case anyway, not in order to air what
knowledge I have of these matters, but because it is the only way

of making reasonably sure that you will talk about the same fish when you meet somebody who lives farther from you than your immediate neighbourhood. English is not the only language that has been used loosely in the naming of fish. The same applies to French, Spanish, Catalan, Italian, Portuguese and my own, Serbo-Croat. I think this recklessness is present in all languages. The common grey mullet (Mugil) has no less than twelve names in the principal Italian dialects and I dare say that there are at least as many further local variants of these. I am sure that the Greeks and Romans were as guilty as we are today. There is an additional difficulty, however. Even the scientists are divided into schools so that one and the same fish may carry several scientific names. At this stage there is nothing that I can do about that except to try and be consistent. Even this has been neither easy nor entirely successful, but I do not pretend to have written a work of science.

By giving my other list of the principal families of fish interesting to spearfishermen in the West Indies I have, to a large extent, dealt with all tropical waters. By adding to this list the scientific names of families that are famous along the more temperate waters of the United States I have, I feel, also covered a range that may be useful to spearfishermen elsewhere.

For much more complete information on fishes known along the Atlantic, Pacific and Gulf coasts of the United States I refer the reader to several well-known scientific studies obtainable in America.

WHERE DO FISH BELONG?

Living creatures, by dispositions invented by one of them—Man—belong to the ANIMAL KINGDOM. The KINGDOM is divided into several PHYLA. A PHYLUM (which is the singular of PHYLA) is a group of related beings next in order below the KINGDOM. One of these PHYLA are the *Chordata,* the possessors of the spinal cord. Other PHYLA (with which we are not concerned here, but which I mention by way of clarification) are *Arthropoda,* the animals whose special characteristic is jointed feet, to which insects, spiders, crustacea, etc. belong, and *Mollusca,* the group of soft-bodied, unsegmented beings (usually in shells) to which limpets, snails, oysters, cuttlefish, etc. belong. We are here concerned with the PHYLUM of *Chordata.* In this PHYLUM there is a further division

A school of inquisitive Crevalle Jacks.
Photograph by Roberto Dei

into CLASSES. We have the CLASS of *Mammalia*, to which we human beings belong, and to which belong other beings the females of which possess breasts (mammae) to feed their young. In this PHYLUM we also have the CLASSES of *Amphibia* (the frogs are an example of these), the *Chondrichthyes* (sharks, rays) and *Osteichthyes* (the bony fishes). There are other CLASSES in this PHYLUM but here we leave them out of reckoning.

Both the *Chondrichthyes* and the *Osteichthyes* are CLASSES which we now pursue in this study. The reader will have stumbled over these two names. The end part of each of these two names is the plural of the Greek word for fish and it is, alas, indispensable. The beginning of the name follows the Greek for cartilage and bone respectively. The first, the cartilaginous fishes, have no true bones at all but have instead cartilage of varying thickness and hardness. The second type have bones.

The Greek word for 'fish' struck the early Greek and Roman Christians as very similar to the first letters of Jesus CHristus Salvator. The result was that the fish was the first universal symbol for Christians, later to be replaced by the Cross.

Further divisions are, of course, necessary and each CLASS is divided into SUBCLASSES.

In the CLASS of *Osteichthyes*, there are three SUBCLASSES. The first SUBCLASS is the *Neopterygii*, the modern bony fishes; then the *Palaepterygii*, of which there are only a few survivors, one of them the sturgeon, and the *Choanichthyes*, in which SUBCLASS belong the lung-fishes which still exist and the famous coelacanth which Dr Smith of South Africa and others have found still to exist. The coelacanth is therefore no missing link, but a survivor in the SUBCLASS of *Choanichthyes* thought until recently to have become extinct.

The SUBCLASSES are divided into ORDERS. ORDERS are sometimes divided into SUBORDERS. ORDERS, or SUBORDERS, where they exist, are divided into FAMILIES. Among the bony fishes this is where we at last get on to familiar ground, if the reader will forgive the pun. We have, for instance, the FAMILY of *Scombridae*, the tuna-type family. Each FAMILY is divided into GENERA (kinds, of which the singular is GENUS). Among the tuna-type family there are several GENERA (the plural of GENUS), such as the bonito, cero, albacore, mackerel and, of course, the tuna. Each GENUS is divided into several SPECIES. This means that there are several types of mackerel, several types of tuna, and so on.

ABOUT NAMES

The scientific name of each SPECIES is usually given in three words. The first word is the name of the GENUS or kind, the second is the name of the SPECIES or type of the GENUS, and the third is the name of the scientist who is acknowledged to be the first to have clearly identified the SPECIES. Often and for practical purposes, the third word, the name of the scientist, is left out. The first two words are either in Latin or Greek or a combination of the two, thus: *corvina nigra*, the black croaker.

These names, both for the GENUS and the SPECIES, usually follow certain patterns. They record some distinguishing characteristic or its original name in Latin or Greek, if the GENUS or even the SPECIES has been clearly identified since classical times.

Some examples are:

(a) Classical names for the GENUS such as *muraena* for the moray, *scomber* for some SPECIES of tuna, *clupea* for the herring.

(b) The appearance of the fish which may remind one of a familiar land animal, such as *vulpes* for fox, *canis* for dog, *lupus* for wolf, are used for the GENUS name.

(c) A part of the body particularly striking, such as *cephalus* for the head, is often used for the SPECIES name.

(d) Another characteristic such as *sclero* for hard, *malacus* for soft, *pseudo* for false, *micro* for small and *macro* for large, is used to identify a particular SPECIES.

(e) The number of a part of the body which happens to be characteristic such as *di* for two, *tetra* for three, *hexa* for six, *deca* for ten, is used for the SPECIES name.

(f) Other characteristics such as *ferox* for fierce, *corrugatus* for lined, *albidus* for white, *argentus* for silvery and *auratus* for golden, is used for the SPECIES name.

The vulgar or national names in different languages are the despair of statisticians. Often the Romance languages—French,

Italian, Spanish and Portuguese—follow the Latin of the old Roman names, but this is not always the case.

English, because it is so widely spoken throughout the world, has suffered more than other languages. Old English names for river fishes and the more common fishes around the British Isles were given all over the world to anything that even approached the old friend at home in looks. We thus have the word bass or perch given to fishes that have nothing much to do with bass and perch. Gradually in this way, each English-speaking area developed its own nomenclature. To try and collate the names given to fish by a Bahamian boatman, a Ceylonese chauffeur or a Brighton fisherman is hilarious fun.

If the reader finds me skating gently over the ice of English nomenclature, I beg him to have a try himself. Though it has little to do with this book I will remind the reader that the English language has generally four words only to describe hundreds of identified species—lobster, crayfish, prawn and shrimp.

PARTS OF THE BODY

It is worth while giving a drawing of a bony fish identifying the parts of the body. The fish shown does not exist in real life. It is a drawing made by scientists to show all the parts which bony fishes may have. (See opposite page).

PERSONAL MATTERS

I shall not dwell on such matters as sex and reproduction which are not of interest to the spearfisherman as such.

SPEED

Dr Smith says that in short spurts fish can swim at fifty kilometres per hour. We spearfishermen know that they can be much faster than that. I have watched my son when he was a little boy try to spear small members of the grouper family, not more than ten centimetres long. From the instant that he fired his spear and in the twinkling of an eye, the fishes darted to a full stop two metres away. They had covered a distance thirteen times their size in a split second. Allowing a tenth of a second, and I think this is liberal,

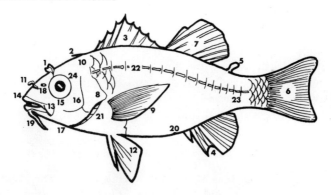

1. Supraorbital tentacle.
2. Horizontal spine before dorsal fin.
3. First dorsal fin.
4. Anal fin, with three spines.
5. Adipose dorsal fin.
6. Caudal fin.
7. Second dorsal fin.
8. Opercle.
9. Pectoral fin.
10. Nape.
11. Nasal tentacle.
12. Pelvic fin.
13. Maxilla.
14. Premaxilla.
15. Cheek.
16. Propercle.
17. Isthmus.
18. Nostril.
19. Mental barbel.
20. Vent.
21. Branchiostegal rays.
22. Lateral line.
23. Caudal peduncle.
24. Adipose eyelid.

the speed is about 110 kilometres per hour. I have seen other fish dash away from me at speeds only a little slower and once a shark disappeared into the blue, frightened by the breaking of a coral rock on to which I was holding, with a speed that matched most race-horses I have seen. Chickens, sparrows and swallows and other birds get out of the way of motor-cars travelling 150 kilometres per hour and I have found that fish have had to learn to get out of the way of spears.

SLEEP

Many fish have been found sleeping, but their sleeping habits have not yet been fully analysed. I have approached Mediterranean croakers in full daylight by surprising them around a rock, and if they were not asleep they gave a good imitation of it for they let my spear tip approach to within thirty centimetres of them.

DRINKING

The fluids of a fish's body contain less salt than sea water but more than fresh water. Dr Bombard survived many days by sucking the fluid out of the flesh of freshly caught fish. Fish take in sea water by mouth and take out of it what they want for life, expelling the remainder through the gills.

TASTE

Some fishes will not take stale bait, some prefer it. The ingenuity of makers of salmon and trout flies seems to know no limits. Presumably the trout is attracted by the appearance of a fly the taste of which it remembers. We know little of the vibrations that may be produced by, say, an old shoe dropped in the water or an attractively smelly saucepan. The fact is that sharks have been known to swallow shoes and saucepans.

VIBRATIONS

There is no question that all fish can feel vibrations. Most probably, their lateral lines are their most sensitive parts. When a fish has been speared and it continues struggling, it will produce entirely different vibration effects on the surrounding water than when it is swimming normally. Sharks and barracuda will appear out of the blue to investigate. Groupers will leave their holes to see what is happening. Even a dead fish, or other device used as bait in trolling will, as it bounces about at the end of its line, attract other fish by the unusual vibrations it causes. It gives the impression of a wounded fish to the undersea world and will be grabbed by a shark, tarpon, marlin, barracuda or any other fish that is able to overtake the bait, moving with the speed of the motor boat.

SMELL

This is also a little-surveyed field. It may be that it is only vibrations caused by the movements of objects in the water which actually attract the fish. This view seems to me more plausible than the view that fish can smell at great distances. The sense of smell must involve particles of the object being in contact with the mucous membrane on the inside of the smeller's nose. Yet I have seen sharks appear when a fish has been wounded before any blood could possibly have reached their noses. They have appeared out of the blue even when no blood had been spilt.

HEARING

Here we are again more or less in the realm of conjecture. Fish undoubtedly react to sounds made both inside and outside the water. An ordinary bell rung under water will scatter most fish. I have seen fish scatter when a spear was dropped to the bottom from a motorboat passing overhead, but I have yet to be convinced that this is not caused by vibrations felt on their body.

SIGHT

Very many fish eat at night and we know that they move about at night without bumping each other or into rocks. They get scared if one waves one's arms about under water and I often feel a fish seems unconcerned if I pretend I am not looking at it. They have eyes and they obviously use them, but again it is difficult to say just how much they rely on them.

TOUCH

People have tickled trout. Many fishes, the mullets or goatfishes, for instance, have barbels with which they find food by touch.

SOUND

I have heard grunts and groupers grunt and others have heard croakers croak. I am sure fishes emit a tremendous variety of sounds which we cannot hear.

LOYALTY

I once came across two large amberjacks. Being anxious to land the bigger, I landed only one instead of the pair. I gathered later that this larger one was the female, and as soon as it had disappeared into the outer world above the surface the male went off. Had I exercised restraint and landed the male first, the female would, I was told, have lingered much longer in the vicinity and I might well have landed the female too. I do not know the moral of this story.

INTELLIGENCE

Fish seem to me to vary tremendously in intelligence looked at from the point of view of the spearfisherman. Wrasse never seem to learn how dangerous we are and this applies to their relatives, the smaller parrot fishes. I have seen many rock-dwelling fish make a fool of me and my companions by the choice of rocks in which they hid. They moved as though to go out one way or the other and finished up by escaping between our legs. Many areas considered to be 'fished out' contain only wary fish. The fish that go in herds scatter when frightened and soon collect again. Sometimes I have thought I had identified the leader but have never been sure. Some herd fish react so quickly that they seem to be obeying a command, but I feel this is probably an illusion caused by the speed of their reaction. Each member turns left or right apparently at the same instant. The leader, if there is one, cannot be identified. If scared, they will dash off in an orderly fashion.

COURAGE

Elsewhere in this Chapter I have described the courage of a cornered grouper. Little ringed sea breams are great spreaders of alarm and they have often spoiled promising rocks for me by dashing about and to all appearances yelling their heads off warning everybody of my approach.

COLOUR AND SHADES

I have not been able to establish whether or not fish react to colour on the spearfisherman. I have worn blue woollen underwear in order to look more like a fish. I wonder who else under water, apart from myself, was fooled? But, of course, the very existence of many coloured fish and the ability of many of them to change colour to obtain protection by being indistinguishable from their surroundings, would show beyond any doubt that fish distinguish between colours and shades.

Two Amberjacks. This also shows a useful rubber dinghy.
Photograph by Roberto Dei

THE MEDITERRANEAN LIST

The sizes and weights given are *average* for adults in this area.

AMBERJACK or YELLOWTAIL, AMBERFISH, (in New Zealand
misnamed KINGFISH, closely related to the AUSTRALIAN
MURRAY COD). *Seriola, Lichia.* Family *Carangidae*; French:
Liche, Sériole; Italian: *Leccia*; Spanish: *Seriola, Sirviola, Palo-
metón*; Portuguese: *Enchova, Charuteiro*.

One metre, fifteen kilogrammes, silver-coloured, sleek, stream-lined, powerful and roving fish, an amber or yellow line all along its body and amber shading above the lateral line, tail tending to amber or yellow. Sometimes mistaken for, and even sold as, tunny. Great fighter. When young, travels in largish group of twenty or thirty, apt to rest under large boats. Although wary, very curious. I once speared and landed a twenty-kilogramme one in the Bahamas just below the surface. It had come out of nowhere just to look at me. Similar experiences in other waters. Could be cornered by astute teamwork. Heavy eating, like tunny.

BASS, SEA, SEA WOLF. *Labrax, Lupus, Morone.* Family *Percidae*; French: *Loup de Mer, Bar*; Italian: *Branzino*; Spanish: *Lubina, Llobaro, Róbalo*; Portuguese: *Robalo.*
The great Mediterranean food fish, though it is found elsewhere. Size sixty centimetres, weight five kilogrammes. Silvery, torpedo-like body. Hunts alone, extremely voracious. Traveller, makes forays among submerged rocks. Behaviour with spearfishermen unpredictable. Sometimes very curious, will approach a still human body, but at other times flies on sight. If followed quietly along a rocky coast, may allow itself to get frightened, will then zigzag until really desperate. Will then dive under rock or dash off at lightning speed but not too far, enabling stalking to be repeated. Sometimes hovers in caves and in danger will make a dash for the open sea. Will try to pull when speared and should be grabbed firmly by the head or eyes or by inserting thumb and forefinger in gills. Excellent eating.

BREAM, SEA, BAMBOO. *Box Salpa.* Subfamily *Boopsinae*; Family *Sparidae*; French: *Saupe*; Italian: *Salpa*; Spanish: *Salema, Salpa*; Portuguese: *Salema.*
Quite my favourite fish, not for eating but because of its en-chanting alternative names. In addition to *Salpa* and *Box* being apparently interchangeable for the scientific genus name and the scientific species name, there is a third *Boops* which has worked its way into various learned works I have consulted in preparing this Chapter. We thus have *Box Boops* as a name and even *Boops Boops*. Who would be cad enough to spear a fish called *Boops Boops*? They are timid little things that seem to get hysterical fits when you blink inside your mask. A typically Mediterranean fish, it has

no recognized English name. Size twenty centimetres, weight half a kilogramme. The yellow stripes all along its body have caused it to be called 'bamboo fish' in South Africa.

BREAM, SEA, GOLDEN. *Chrysophrys* or *Aurata*. Subfamily *Sparinae*; Family *Sparidae*; French: *Daurade, Dorée*; Italian: *Orata*; Spanish: *Dorada*; Portuguese: *Dourada*.

Golden coloured. Size forty centimetres, weight two-and-a-half kilogrammes. Alleged to prefer saltier waters. Fairly peaceful fish. Keeps its distance from other fish, and the spearfisherman may surprise it feeding on molluscs inshore or inside rocks. Very difficult to spear when moving off into open water. Excellent eating.

BREAM, SEA, MARBLE. *Pagellus*. Subfamily *Pagellinae*; Family *Sparidae*; French: *Pageau marbré*; Italian: *Pagello, Marmora*; Spanish: *Pagel, Breca Mabre*; Portuguese: *Bica, Bezugo*.

Reddish or pinkish. Size up to thirty centimetres, weight half a kilogramme. Good sport for the beginner. Should be given up as soon as spearfisherman has any experience. Lives on sandy sea bottoms and among weeds. Quiet, inoffensive member of the underwater community. Good eating.

BREAM, SEA, RINGED. *Oblata*. Family *Sparidae*; French: *Oblade*; Italian: *Occhiata*; Spanish: *Oblada, Doblada*; Portuguese: *Dobrada*.

A small, timid, quick, lead-blue-grey fish with a black ring at the narrow part forward of the caudal fin. Keeps well into the rocky shore or among weeds, and near ports; too small for any spearfisherman of experience, but as it is excellent food, good sport for the beginner. Stalking roughly equivalent to stalking butterflies. Size twenty centimetres, weight quarter of a kilogramme. As they are such excellent sport for anglers off rocky shores, the spearfisherman should leave them in peace.

BREAM, SEA, STRIPED. *Sargus*. Subfamily *Sparinae*; Family *Sparidae*; French: *Sargue, Sard, Sparaillon*; Italian: *Sargo, Sparaglione*; Spanish: *Sardo, Sargo, Raspalton, Vidriada*; Portuguese: *Sargo*.

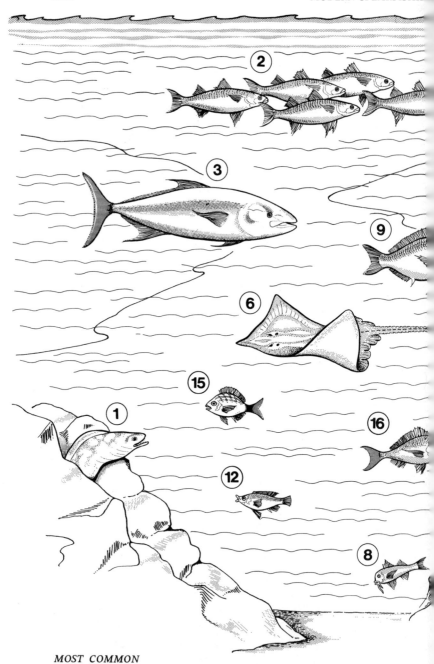

MOST COMMON
MEDITERRANEAN FISHES. (1) Moray. (2) Grey mullet. (3) Amberjack.
(4) Octopus. (5) Grouper. (6) Stingray. (7) Bamboo sea bream. (8) Red mullet

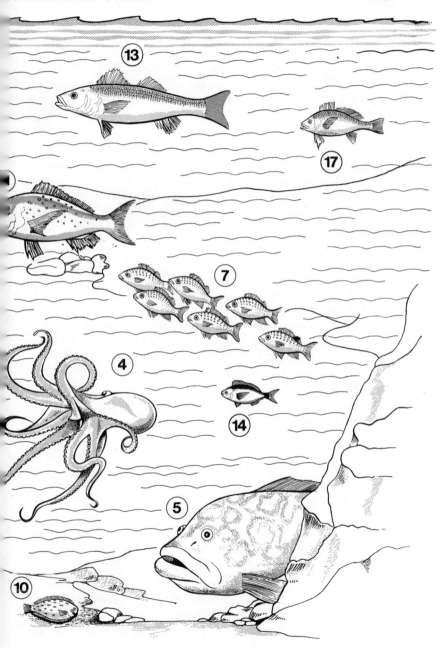

(9) Golden sea bream. (10) Sole. (11) Dentex. (12) Wrasse. (13) Sea wolf. (14) Ringed sea bream. (15) Striped sea bream. (16) Pink sea bream. (17) Marble sea bream.

Never leaves the coast, does not move very far from his little holes in the rocks. Silvery, about thirty centimetres long, weight one kilogramme, with black vertical stripes. Timid, rarely curious. If you keep very close to the steep rocky shore wall he will sometimes rush up at you from the depths to inspect you. Stalking techniques in the text. There is a close relative with a more pointed mouth, which has similar habits but prefers open water. Latin: *Charax*; French: *Charax*; Italian: *Corace*; Spanish: *Variada.**

CONGER EEL. *Conger*. Family *Congridae*; French: *Congre*; Italian: *Grongo*; Spanish: *Congrio*; Portuguese: *Congro*.

Absence of scales, teeth form cutting edge, snakelike, colour varies from light grey to black. Has pectoral fins, unlike moray. Size up to two metres, weight seven kilogrammes. Lives in rocks. When seen should be speared just behind the head or below the mouth, and only if shot is a certain bull. Should be held tight with thumb and finger in gills pressing the body through which the spear has been pushed against wings of spear point. The muzzle of the gun may be inserted in its mouth. The celebrated Dr Smith of South Africa gives an explanation: 'A large live Conger landed into a small boat in a rough sea by an inexperienced amateur created a situation of intense action.' Not as dangerous as a moray, but can be vicious when wounded. Considered good eating, but not by me. In a boat it should, like the moray, have a spare fish ring passed through one gill and mouth and the ring passed round a fixed place in the boat and then snapped closed.

CROAKER. *Corvina*. Family *Sciaenidae*; French: *Corbeau*; Italian: *Corvo*; Spanish: *Corvina*; Portuguese: *Roncador*.

Size thirty centimetres, weight two kilogrammes. Brownish violet, coppery lustre, light coloured below almost white, and with rather full white lips. A typical Mediterranean fish, usually floats quietly on the shady side of rocks or in caves in company of five or six others. Dives for cover at last moment and will then stay hidden and frightened for a long time. Does not fight. Good eating.

DENTEX (no English name). *Dentex*. Family *Denticidae*; French:

*Note: I have deliberately left out the Pink Sea Bream (*Pagrus* Family *Sparidae*), a fish common enough in the Mediterranean but very difficult to spear for the beginner. Behaves rather like the Golden Sea Bream. (Illustrated page 152–3.)

Denti, Denté; Italian: *Dentice*; Spanish: *Denton, Dentol*; Portuguese: *Dentex*.

Size fifty centimetres, weight seven kilogrammes. Silvery-blue, fairly large head, canine teeth, predatory. Mainly in deep water. Will make forays into shallow water. Almost impossible to spear alone, but with teamwork described in text it is possible to corner him. Fights hard. Excellent eating. A typical Mediterranean fish.

FLATFISHES, principal Mediterranean species. *Rhombus* or *Bothus* and *Solea*. Families *Bothidae, Pleuronectidae* and *Soleidae*; French: *Poissons plats, Sole*; Italian: *Sogliola, Rombo*; Spanish: *Solla, Rodaballo, Lenguado*; Portuguese: *Solha*.

These fishes are variable in form all over the world and anyone apart from systematists would have a rough time in differentiating among them. Some call those with both eyes on the left side, flounders, and those with eyes on the right side, soles. In the UK the right-eyeds include halibut, dab, plaice and the soles, while the left side claims the turbot and the brill. Sometimes, just to confuse the matter, the right-sided occur in species in which most are left-sided and vice versa. Flatfishes may be an unimaginative and too general term for the expert, but for present purposes it is adequate. The flatfishes are in an ORDER apart from the others and are found in most seas. The adult has become asymmetrical, both eyes being on one side. The two sides of flatfish also differ in colour and nature of scales, as well as some other minor ways. They generally lie flat on the sand with only their eyes visible and the rest of their bodies barely discernible. They are very slow and are easy targets. Most of the flatfish make excellent eating.

GROUPER, GARRUPA, ROCK COD, ROCKFISH, BLACK SEA BASS, ROCK HIND, HAMLET, JEWFISH, SEA PERCH. *Epinephelus, Serranus*. Family *Serranidae*: French: *Mérou*; Italian: *Cernia*; Spanish: *Mero*; Portuguese: *Garoupa, Mero*.

Size one metre, weight ten kilogrammes. There are a tremendous number of species, belonging to a considerable number of genera, of this family in all warm waters. That is why I have given so many names in English. Except for size, which varies from a few centimetres to about 500 kilogrammes in weight, the general description of the Mediterranean *epinephelus* is valid for all, although the names overlap a great deal. Robust body, large head, large mouth with small teeth in bands in jaws, on the palate and on the gills. There is in the Mediterranean a species more streamlined and mobile, greenish in colour and not a great fighter. Inhabits particular rocks, looks like a rough rock, never moves far, often found apparently sitting down, body at forty-five degrees, looking curiously upwards at spearfisherman. Stalking described in text. In the Mediterranean considered the great prize among spearfishermen. To kill your first grouper is like making your first million; the others are much easier. Usually alone, very careful, but curiosity sometimes kills him. Mostly below ten metres. Must be hit between the eyes, or at least somewhere in the head. If hit elsewhere on the body, he will bury himself in a rock hole and hold himself fast to rocks with his fins and mouth, and cannot be dislodged until nearly dead. For sheer bravery against patently overwhelming odds it is equal to Spanish fighting bulls. Feeds on fish and molluscs, but octopus is specially favoured food. I would rather be photographed with a grouper, fairly fought and landed, than with any other fish. In years to come, when landlubbers become acquainted with life under the sea, the strength of a grouper relative to its size will become legendary. Good eating when not larger than ten kilogrammes. Head bones, tail and fins help to make superb fish soup. I am afraid that the grouper's generally accepted name, which stems from the Portuguese name for one genus, *Garoupa*, is not a happy choice. It gives the impression of representing a cowardly, sheeplike animal that seeks safety in large numbers. The grouper is usually the very opposite of this. The Carribean name Hamlet also conjures up visions of the sweet Prince and takes us away from the right track. If Jewfish is a corruption of Jawfish, it is bad. If it is an expression of anti-Semitism because of the fishes' ugly appearance, it is worse. Altogether an animal unfortunately named, because bass, perch and cod are names given to other fish too. I like the Spanish, Mero. It sounds a little like Toro—a bull. I should dearly love to call groupers Bulls or Sea Bulls.

MORAY EEL, or ROMAN EEL, MORAY. *Muraena*. Family *Muraenidae*; French: *Murène*; Italian: *Murena*; Spanish: *Morena*; Portuguese: *Moreia*.

The celebrated Roman eel has no pectoral fins and is usually speckled brownish-yellow on black. Vicious teeth. The larger species appear to be among the most dangerous of all marine creatures and are much dreaded by divers. I have never known one to attack, but putting one's hand blindly inside rocks may be considered by the moray to be an attack on it. I have speared many in the Mediterranean and elsewhere. It is the only fish that has attempted to bite me when speared. When speared, it should be treated even more gingerly than the conger, described above, and only, I repeat only, shot when success is almost certain. See the use of the knife with morays in Chapter 3. More often than not, it hides inside rocks with its head and neck swaying about outside, starry-eyed, breathing as though in agony and gasping its last breath. Up to one metre long, weight five kilogrammes. In spite of its smooth muscular body, its flesh is very light and it is an excellent fish to eat.

MULLET, GREY or SPRINGER. *Mugil*. Family *Mugilidae*; French: *Mulet gris, Muge*; Italian: *Muggine*; Spanish: *Mújol, Lisa*; Portuguese: *Tainha*.
These timid, torpedo-shaped grey fishes are related, of all fish, to what Dr Smith calls 'perhaps the most ferocious of all living fishes'—the barracuda. They swim in or near the surface of the water. They do not take bait and only nibble at weeds or scoop up mud or slimy sand. Usually appear where fresh water is near, or in or near ports. Size thirty centimetres, weight one kilogramme. Stalking described in Chapter 4. Only fair eating.

MULLET, RED, GOATFISH. *Mullus*. Family *Mullidae*; French: *Rouget, Surmullet*; Italian: *Barbone, Triglia*; Spanish: *Salmonete*; Portuguese: *Salmonete*.
Pinkish, usually with a darkish line along its body but the pink appears only out of the water. Two long barbels on the chin with which the red mullet burrows in the sand. Size twenty-five centimetres, weight a quarter of a kilogramme. A well-known fish in the Mediterranean, where they are rightly famed as food when fresh. They do not appear to see very well; run off in a panic along the bottom from which they never stray far. They seem to stop for breath every few metres and choose to lie low in a place where they think they are not seen. As soon as the spearfisherman is modestly skilful, he should not shoot unless the fish is moving. Should be shot in the head only, because of its most fragile body.

OCTOPUS. *Octopus.* French: *Pulpe*; Italian: *Polpo*; Spanish: *Pulpo*; Portuguese: *Polvo*.

Who does not know this illustrious figure whose legendary achievements have spread its fame all over the dry lands? Except in water too deep for the ordinary spearfisherman and excluding some coral reefs of the Pacific, and especially in Puget Sound, the octopus is a fairly small genus of cephalopod mollusc. Its tentacles are usually shorter than the arm of an adult human. It can only bite a little with its small beak on the middle of its under-side and is not poisonous to touch. If held tightly it cannot escape nor possibly do any harm. It is disgusting and slimy to touch but should be grabbed with the hand, and not speared. If speared, it may succeed in working itself off even when several barbs are in it. When frightened, it will seek to hide its path of retreat by shooting a jet of black liquid towards the aggressor. This will form a little cloud which will stay long enough to allow the octopus to retreat and pretend to be a round stone. Four shots of its ink will exhaust its supply. The safest way of preventing it from moving (short of biting it between the eyes—the traditional way of killing an octopus but difficult when using a snorkel)—is to turn the sack, which is its body, inside out. The tentacles do not suck your blood but help it to hold on to you. If left long on your skin they will leave red marks showing that your blood has been pulled to the spot where its suckers were. If women and children are about, there is no better or easier way of establishing a reputation for bravery and a name as a man of the sea than by diving and grabbing one of these poor creatures and bringing it in, clinging to your chest. It adds much to fish soup but the tentacles when cooked still feel very rubbery to eat. See the American and West Indies list for further comments.

RAY. There are many families belonging to the ORDER of *Rajae* (*skates and rays*) which itself belongs to the SUBCLASS of *Euselachii* (*sharks and rays*). The latter is one of the SUB-CLASSES of the CLASS of *chondrichthyes*, the rather difficult scientific name for cartilaginous fishes. All the other fish described in the Mediterranean list (except, of course, the octopus which is not a fish) belong to the CLASS of *osteichthyes*, i.e. bony fishes.

See also the American and West Indies list for further comments.

Even though rays are not that numerous in the Mediterranean, it is worth while beginning to swim very soon off sandy beaches not usually used by bathers. Tramping about on the sand without looking is the best way of stepping on a ray, which will only start whipping about when it imagines it is being attacked.

Among the fish in the ORDER of *Rajae*, I shall dwell on three Mediterranean species only, warning the reader interested in more details that there is much more to all this.

(a) STINGRAY or WHIPRAY. *Trygon, Dasyatis.* Family *Trigonidae* or *Dasyatidae*; French: *Raie pastenague*; 'Italian: *Trigone, Pastinaca*; Spanish: *Raya, Pastinaca*; Portuguese: *Ratão.* The celebrated species is the *Trygon Pastinacus*, hence the alternate name in the Romance languages.

Brownish violet in colour, the body can be two metres long with the wings the same width, weight thirty kilogrammes. A triangular or rounded body, a hump in the centre goes all down its back giving it a more bulky appearance than the rays of the *raiidae* or *aetobatidae* families. Small teeth and no dorsal fin. A long tail and a serrated venomous spine well behind and below the base of the tail. The skin is alleged to be covered with a poisonous mucus, but I have handled the Mediterranean stingray with no ill effects. I once speared one and it turned out, to my horror, to be an expectant mother. She produced in my dinghy eight leaden-grey, velvety cigars which unfolded into babies as they appeared one by one, tails three times as long as their bodies. They swam away, eight little orphans, into their blue world and I swore I would never spear another one.

It will not attack unprovoked but a wound inflicted by the formidable spine is venomous (see text on venomous fish in Chapter 7). The death of Ulysses was supposedly to have been caused by a spear with such a spine, and many stories have survived the centuries to serve as a warning.

If you must spear one, shoot from above coming from the back or from the side aiming at the eye. Give enough line to allow the pastenague to be at least three metres away from you. It will either try to pull round a rock, which may break your line, or try to bury itself in the sand. Get out of the water first as you have no means of getting near the fish without coming within the range of the spine, which by that time will be whipping in all directions.

When you have the fish out on a flat surface, step on the tail, having placed some non-slipping material between the sole of your foot and the slippery tail. Step far enough down the tail to avoid the spine. The moment you are firmly on the tail the fish is helpless. Then cut the spine off with a shaving motion up and towards the base of the spine. Bury or otherwise destroy the spine completely. The fish will not even try to whip after that. Poor eating.

(b) ELECTRIC RAY or NUMBFISH, SHOCKFISH. *Torpedo.* Family *Torpedinidae*; French: *Torpille*; Italian: *Torpedine*; Spanish: *Tremielga, Tremoló*; Portuguese: *Dormideira.*

An electric ray of sixty centimetres can produce a strong electric shock. Viviparous, flabby and circular. Two electric organs, one on each side of the body, but the electric supply is easily exhausted. Sluggish, but can live long out of water. Poor eating. Stalking and spearing as with the stingray. 'How did they manage before electricity was discovered?' my friend Eric Weinmann asked.

(c) SKATE, RAY, sometimes THORNBACK. *Raia.* Family *Raiidae*; French: *Raie*; Italian: *Razza*; Spanish: *Raya*; Portuguese: *Raia.*

Lives rather more deeply and quietly than the stingray. Oviparous, producing eggs in large horny rectangular cases, no whip, two dorsal fins. They vary greatly and scientists constantly promise fuller analysis and classification, but this is very difficult. Only fair eating. Same manner of stalking and spearing as the stingray.

WRASSE or RAINBOW FISH. *Labrus.* Family *Labridae*; French: *Tanche*; Italian: *Labride*; Spanish: *Tordo, Grivia*; Portuguese: *Truta.*

There are about five hundred species of the *Labridae* identified all over the world. Size up to thirty centimetres long, weight half to one kilogramme. Thick white lips. Mouth can be extended. Distinguished by an almost infinite variety of colouring. In Northern waters they are the most brilliantly coloured fishes. They live in and about rocks and reefs and in seaweed. Some are herbivorous but most are carnivorous, feeding also on molluscs, crushing them with their round teeth which, however, often include canines. The most common in the Mediterranean are the bluish-green, green and red-orange-black speckled. They move slowly in shallow water, the bluish-green often found feeding in a vertical position, head upwards. Will not fight hard. Not very good eating, very soft flesh.

NORTH AMERICA AND THE WEST INDIES LIST
(To be read in conjunction with the Mediterranean fishes)

ANGEL and BUTTERFLY FISHES. Family *Chaetodontidae*
I mention these but beg readers not to spear them. Fairly small, slow, deep-bodied but thin with a single dorsal fin, they are absolute sitters for anyone but a drowning man. There are angelfish

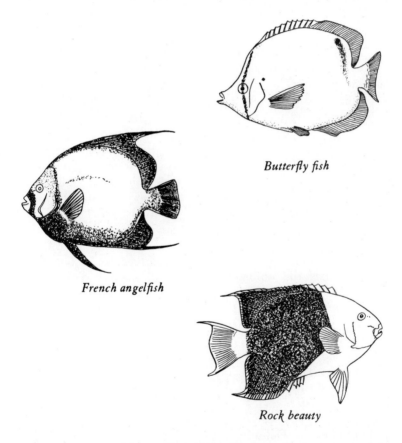

Butterfly fish

French angelfish

Rock beauty

all over the tropical seas off coral reefs where they are one of the elements that make up the beauty of the reefs. They are not really good to eat so there is no excuse whatever for spearing them. The moment they realize you are not after them, they will swim about you tamely.

The great barracuda

BARRACUDA. Family *Sphyraenidae*

The legendary reputation of a barracuda is just a lot of nonsense. To illustrate the power of fishermen's stories coupled with the landlubbers' credulity about unknown phenomena, I must give the reader the following silly story. Even Dr J. L. B. Smith, of Rhodes University, Grahamstown, South Africa, the world's most eminent authority on fish and the celebrated discoverer of the coelacanth considers these 'tigers of the sea', as he calls them, to be, perhaps, the most ferocious animals on earth.

The first barracuda I met was in 1949 in the Bahamas. It seemed to confirm everything Dr Smith and the legend fabricators had said. I was fishing very near the shore in fairly shallow water. Suddenly I noticed a barracuda swimming slowly around me and watching me with its great eyes. I had been told that barracuda only showed black spots when they were asleep. This one was, unfortunately, not asleep in spite of several large black spots on its side. Allowing for the distortion of the lens of my mask and the sea water, I judged it to be about 130 centimetres in length. The barracuda has the unfortunate habit of opening its mouth as though it was barking. This gave me a good chance to see its much vaunted teeth. I had discussed barracuda with friends in Nassau during the few days previously and the consensus of opinion was that a barracuda would not attack a human being although most people still continued to fear them. I had also been told that if I had a fish on my fish ring, the barracuda might be tempted to go for the fish because it had smelled blood. I was assured, however, that a barracuda was only dangerous in the sense that animals were thought to be dangerous if they were willing to defend themselves.

Encouraged by remembering this advice, I began slowly approaching the barracuda. I was disconcerted to discover that it made no attempt whatever to swim away. It remained perfectly still and continued to watch me carefully. I even tried to make one or two violent movements with my hand. Still the barracuda stood its ground. It presented an almost perfect target by the time my gun was about 130 centimetres away. But then I began to think. Suppose a barracuda can move very quickly and I miss—what will happen? What if all my friends were wrong? I shall be utterly helpless if it should then choose to attack me and, even if it should find it impossible to eat me, it was perfectly clear that it could bite me very hard. I had to keep very near the surface in order to be able to breathe. I obviously could not swim as fast as the barracuda. I should probably lose my spear, lose my gun and, of course, my dignity.

I immediately sacrificed my dignity. I changed my mind and started swimming away, but by this time I had become sufficiently impressed by the barracuda not to dare to turn my back to it and swim the crawl, which would have been the fastest method of retreating. I remained with my face towards it, and lying on my back, I used the back-crawl stroke with my legs and my one free arm. I started edging away but remained facing the fish. To my consternation the barracuda began following me. By then I had really become frightened. My brother was spearfishing near by and I hoped that I might attract his attention and that he would come near me and splash about the water and frighten the barracuda. Then I realized that with my snorkel in my mouth I could not shout and I dared not take my eyes off the fish. I edged away slowly and managed to increase the distance between the barracuda and myself to about three metres. As I came nearer the shore the barracuda finally gave up following me. At no stage did it show any sign of belligerence—it simply remained quite unfrightened of me.

I showed, I think, all the reactions which a beginner would exhibit in such circumstances. I tell this story because this is a handbook for beginners. My advice to any beginner who meets a barracuda is to leave it alone.

There is no doubt that, if you left your feet dangling over the side of a boat in waters where barracuda are known to appear, you could run the risk of being bitten. If you waded in shallow water you might also be bitten. Barracuda will attack and are willing to take chunks out of bodies much bigger than themselves. This much is known and accepted, even by me, about barracuda.

Since this first experience I have come across very many barracuda. I no longer run home. I speared a muttonfish once in the presence of a barracuda. The fish wriggled off my spear and hid under a small rock five metres deep so that both the barracuda and I could still see it. I slowly loaded my gun again, dived and hit my fish properly this time. The barracuda made no move. He simply watched me from about six metres away. I pulled in my line and handed the spear to the man in the boat, watching the barracuda all the time.

Later I took courage and decided to be aggressive with barracuda. When I made as though to spear them in earnest and not as on my first encounter, they retreated. Then I became ambitious and shot one. I hit it in the gills but failed to hold it. It managed to open its gills wide enough when pulling away and wrenched itself off my spear. I could not get near it again before it disappeared into the blue.

Since then I have speared many barracuda and landed them. They fight hard to get away but, if carefully handled, cannot bite the spearfisherman.

Barracuda will not be frightened off by shouting. Splashing on the surface with an oar does keep them off, but will not drive them away. On the other hand I have been in the water many times with four or five barracuda circling round me. Once I counted thirty. It is always a thrill, though they have all in fact left me alone, simply gazing at me from a respectful distance.

A courageous animal that has so far had it all its own way, the barracuda may in the end become the greatest and finest sport for the fisherman. The element of fear will always be present when Man meets the 'tiger of the seas' in the tiger's own world. There are few thrills so deep and memorable as the thrill of fear. Men fight and kill the noble and savage bulls of Spain. To allow for the advantages their brains have given them in the way of weapons, they have invented an elaborate code of manners which they must obey in the bullring. I hope that we will have the decency to establish some conventions about fighting and killing barracuda only with a handspear. For the sake of ourselves it is worth treating this brave and graceful animal with the dignity it deserves. Thus the barracuda may not come to be treated the way some big game are on land.

The barracuda can reach two metres in length, has an elongated, cylindrical body, widely separated dorsal fins, long snout, lower jaw projecting and mouth often showing three large pointed teeth.

Should not be stalked without a boat, and it is inadvisable to fire unless one is certain of a shot in the gills or just behind them. In Chapter 4 I have described the most useful way of holding on to large fish that are willing and able to fight hard for liberty. I am always told that the black spots on its body appear only from time to time, and they are said by various observers to appear when the fish is (a) young, (b) asleep, (c) angry. I have seen many barracuda, all with spots, and they were never asleep, seldom angry and only sometimes young. Always lean and hungry-looking, and though it does not think politically, the barracuda should not be considered undangerous. I saw one go for the fin of a friend of mine who was struggling with a fish. In its excitement it could not tell the difference between his fins and the speared fish. Its cousin, the European sea pike, is seldom ferocious. In the Mediterranean, Madeira and off Africa's Atlantic coast, and in the Red Sea, its young appear in large groups. Considered by many, especially in Ceylon, to be good eating, but not by me.

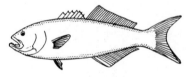

Bluefish

BLUEFISH. Family *Pomatomidae*
   This family bears some resemblance to the jacks, but it is in fact quite distinct. Some bluefish reach twelve kilogrammes. They are widely spread all over the warm seas and they migrate along the United States Atlantic coasts up and down from Massachusetts to Florida. They travel in large schools and are very voracious. Considered excellent food.

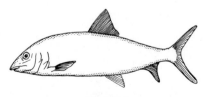

Bonefish

BONEFISH. Family *Albalidae*
   This family, of which the bonefish is the most widely known

species among game fishermen, belongs to the ORDER of *Iso-spondyli* to which herrings, smelts and anchovies belong. A silvery-coloured fish which tends to enter estuaries in large numbers. Sometimes sixty centimetres long. The island of Andros in the Bahamas is famous bonefish territory, but its habitat is the entire Atlantic coast of the United States. It is also known on the Pacific side.

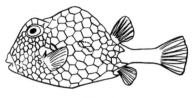

Trunkfish

BOXFISHES. Family *Ostraciontidae*

The boxfishes, trunkfishes, cofferfishes or cowfishes belong to an ORDER of several families where the body is encased in body plates of cartilage, fused to form a solid box. They have no speed so spearing them is no sport at all. By the time I succeeded in opening the only specimen I ever speared, I was too ashamed and ill-tempered to remember to try and eat one.

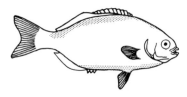

Bermuda chub

CHUBS. Family *Kyphosidae*

The best-known name is the Bermuda chub. Known north as far as Cape Cod, and fairly common off Florida, Bermuda, the Bahamas, Haiti and Jamaica and elsewhere in the West Indies. Steel grey in colour with darker fins. Deep, compressed body almost perfectly oval. Dashes in and out of reef holes and among stones in the churned-up waters off rocky shores, mainly in shallow waters. Sometimes they come in great numbers. They do not move in military formation but keep more or less together acting as individuals. Sometimes shows spots. Rudderfish is another name given to the chub, as it has been known to follow closely behind ships for many miles. Feeds on marine plants and small creatures. Flesh not esteemed. Grows to forty-five centimetres. Not to be confused with the many small fresh-water chubs.

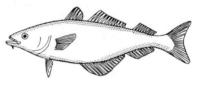

Pollack

CODS and POLLACKS. Family *Gadidae*

Both belong to the cod family. The pollack is widely known on both sides of the Atlantic, but keeps to the colder waters. Unlike other cods, the pollack will go very close to shore and thus belongs to this classification which is for spearfishermen. Has been known to reach over fifteen kilogrammes but the average size is well below this.

CONGER EELS. Family *Congridae*

The description of the Mediterranean variety is valid here. Well-known in American waters.

Croaker

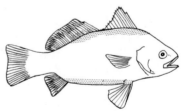

Silver perch

CROAKERS and DRUMS. Family *Sciaenidae*

A large family known all over the warm and temperate waters of the world. Well represented along Atlantic and Pacific coasts of the United States. A safe way of identifying them, since their characteristics and special names are very varied, is the lateral line which is continuous and extends all the way to the caudal fin. Some have small barbels on the lower jaw. They can make a croaking noise, sometimes thought to sound like the beating of a distant drum.

Well-known fish in this family are the silver perch (not a member of the perch family), the various drums (banded, black, red and star), the Atlantic croakers, whitings and ribbonfish.

They inhabit the shallower waters off sandy beaches and are often in the surf or kelp. They feed on shrimps, crabs and the small fishes. Usually up to thirty centimetres long.

They are relatively easy shots and do not fight much when speared.

Dolphin

DOLPHINS. Family *Coryphaenidae*

Unmistakable shape. In large males the forehead is very prominent, giving it a curious bulging forehead. Its dorsal fin starts on the head itself. A great traveller, the dorado, as it is also often known to prevent confusion with the mammal dolphins, is perhaps the most widely dispersed game fish of the world. They are known to travel dozens of miles per day and the members of the Kon-Tiki expedition found them their most constant companions. Dr Bombard, who sailed alone in a rubber life raft across the Atlantic, was followed for weeks by one particular dolphin he named Dora. In Hawaii this fish goes under the fascinating name of Mahi-mahi.

Will fight hard, and the spearfisherman should treat this splendid fish as he does amberjacks and tuna.

FLATFISHES. Order *Heterosomata*

Same general data as Mediterranean list. In the Western Hemisphere an alternative name to those already mentioned in plate fishes.

GOATFISHES. Family *Mullidae*

General description and illustration in the Mediterranean list. Always swim slowly along sea bottoms. Two long chin barbels stir up the sand in search for food. While the Mediterranean variety is exclusively pinkish, the West Indian goatfishes have many colours—yellow, red, violet, blue and green. Easy shot. Excellent food. Grows to twenty centimetres.

GROUPERS or SEA BASSES. Family *Serranidae*

The Mediterranean variety have been described and the many English names given and commented upon. Here I list them under their most common American names. There are, as in the Mediterranean, two main divisions all over the world. The same general characteristics apply as in the Mediterranean list to the warm-water sea bass, groupers or rockfish, as they are chiefly called in America and the West Indies. The two genera which have the largest number of species identified are the *Epinephelus* and *Mycteroperca*. One division has a rather smaller head and more streamlined, narrow body and pointed face with eyes near each other and lower lip protruding, and are rather more mobile. In the West Indies the chief species of this more mobile kind are the blackfin or black rockfish and the yellowfin rockfish, the former being allegedly poisonous to eat in most areas. I have defied this superstition and am alive to tell the story. The other division with fatter body and relatively rounder and larger head like Mediterranean grouper, can be cornered more easily, but will fight harder. The famous Nassau grouper belongs here. Stalking and shooting and other characteristics described in the Mediterranean list. Groupers abound under their various names in both oceans surrounding the United States.

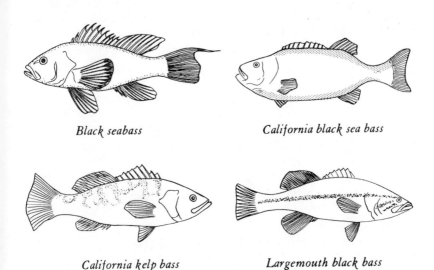

Black seabass   *California black sea bass*

California kelp bass   *Largemouth black bass*

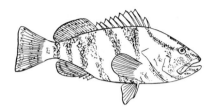

Nassau grouper

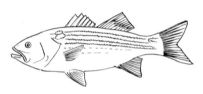

Striped bass

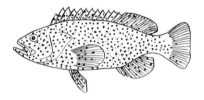

Rock hind

The smaller black sea bass (*Centropristes striatus*) which inhabits greater depths in great numbers, both on the American and the European and African coasts of the Atlantic, should not be confused with the lone black grouper of the Florida and Caribbean waters nor with the black jewfish known also in California as the California black sea bass (*Stereolepis gigas*), both of which attain enormous size. In California, the California kelp bass and the sand bass are both closely related to the better-known groupers. The striped bass is perhaps the best-known North Atlantic representative of this family.

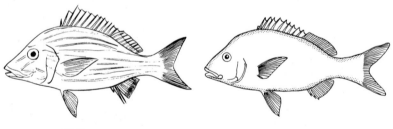

Yellow grunt   *Margate fish*

GRUNTS. Family *Haemuliae*

The grunts grow to about thirty centimetres in length. On the one side they are related to the snappers and on the other to the porgies (the West Indian and American name for the *Sparidae* family). Their habits are similar to both. Several genera very common in Bermuda and elsewhere in the West Indies. Quiet, unobtrusive, fairly timid, they inhabit coral reefs. The white, the yellow, and the blue-striped are very common as are the rather larger margate fish and grey grunt. When pulled out into the air they make a slight grunting noise. I have heard grunts make this noise under water when speared or frightened.

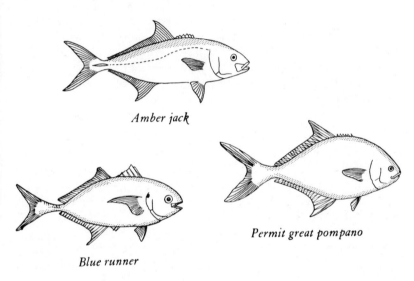

Amber jack

Permit great pompano

Blue runner

JACKS, KINGFISHES, POMPANO, AMBERJACKS.
Family *Carangidae*.

Some ichthyologists separate the family into two—the *Carangidae* and *Seriolidae*, and I find that in this large and rather diversified group of fishes there is considerable confusion both in scientific and in English names.

1. *The Caranxes or Jacks.* The *Caranx latus* is called horse-eyed jack by most and yellow jack by others, while the further description of cavalle or crevalle jack would indicate that its horse-type eye is its accepted distinguishing mark. The *Caranx hippos* (Greek for 'horse') is called common jack by some and crevalle, presumably a corruption of cheval jack, by others. The other two very common jacks are first the *Caranx crysos*, the blue runner or hardtail jack as it is also called, and secondly, the *Caranx ruber*. The runner is

related to the blue runner, which of all the jacks has the greatest number of lateral scutes. The scutes, or enlarged lateral keeled plates, help these fast-moving but very narrow fish to keep an even keel. These are the smallest, though most common, of the jacks, only rarely growing to sixty centimetres in length. They feed on small fishes and are extremely voracious.

The jacks and others under this heading frequent most warm seas and the Western Atlantic but reach well up the Eastern shore of the United States and down to central Brazil. I have most often seen the smaller jacks of all varieties in schools of twenty or thirty, and have occasionally been surrounded by hundreds, not knowing at which one to fire. Most of the jacks will go out of their way to inspect spearfishermen, but one shot, whether successful or not, is enough to make them go off never to return. When speared, they flutter hard on the spear, and it is this type of flutter (accompanied by some vibration unobservable by us) that often brings a shark out of the blue. Although their flesh is surprisingly compact for such a relatively small fish, I find the smaller jacks most satisfying to eat when grilled. In South Africa, most of the jacks are called kingfishes by Dr Smith.

2. *The Seriolas or Amberjacks.* Four main species of the amberjack are known in the Atlantic. They keep to the warmer waters. The Pacific *Seriola dorsalis* is called yellowtail. The amberjack grows larger than the other jacks. In the oceans, they often go about in pairs. It is a typical migratory fish, fast-moving, strong and voracious. Big-game fishermen are particularly impressed by its fighting qualities. Grows up to fifty kilogrammes and 150 centimetres. It has an amber band from its eye to the base of the caudal fin, hence the name amberjack or amberfish.

It is curious enough to come quite near and only a quick and decisive shot will have any chance. This can be achieved either by staying quite still and not even turning towards the fish if it comes from the side, or by slowly lowering oneself below the surface by almost imperceptible movements of the free hand. The spear itself (the line is probably not strong enough) should be grabbed immediately in both hands if possible and the index finger and thumb inserted in the gills the moment the fish is near enough. Then comes the struggle described in Chapter 4.

3. *Trachinotus or Pompano.* In Hawaii, goes under the name of *Ulua*, and in South Africa it is also called ladyfish, while in Ceylon

it is called queenfish. Big ones have been landed both in the Pacific and the Atlantic. Jack Ackerman's technique of stalking is described in Chapter 4. In Ceylon and elsewhere in the Indian Ocean where they can reach thirty-five kilogrammes they come rushing in to the reefs in the surging waters before sundown as the waves break over the reefs. Only brief glimpses are possible in the agitated sea and quick work is essential. Rodney Jonklaas of Ceylon is probably the world's greatest expert in spearing and also in classifying these fishes.

Green moray

MORAY EELS. Family *Muraenidae*

The description of the Mediterranean variety is valid here also. The Mediterranean peoples, not so well acquainted with sharks and having little knowledge of the barracuda, have given the moray eel pride of place among the ferocious fish. In tropical waters there is a green species, but the more common variety is the speckled moray. It is hardly ever seen swimming. When it does it moves like a snake. It is usually to be found inside rocks with only its head and upper part showing. It will not attack unprovoked but it looks hideous and its teeth, always visible, command respect. It may easily try and snap at your hand if you start poking about blindly in a dark hole. It will only do this out of self-defence and if it cannot run away or withdraw deeper into its hole. No creature should be underestimated when it imagines itself to be in the last stages of self-defence. It will then go to the limits of its power like other creatures, from the wasp stinging to Napoleon marching on Moscow. The moray's venomous bite is discussed in Chapter 6, but here it may be said that the beginner had better play safe and avoid it.

Jack Ackerman spears a small fish with his Hawaiian sling and leaves the fish outside a rock where he has seen a moray hiding. He then dives down again with another spear and spears the moray as it lunges forward to bite into the fish. Ackerman has found that the moray is taken out of the water more easily if something is inserted into its mouth to keep its teeth busy and away from himself. A stick, the end of the gun or the knife will all serve this purpose. I have described this technique in Chapter 4.

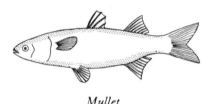

Mullet

MULLETS. Family *Mugilidae*

The Mediterranean variety has been described. The names of some of the Western Hemisphere species are striped mullet, mullet and fan-tailed mullet. Unlike the Mediterranean variety, these silvery fish move up and down the Atlantic coast of the United States in huge numbers. The striped mullet is nearest to its Mediterranean cousin.

Rainbow parrot fish

PARROT FISHES. Family *Sparisomidae* and *Scaridae*

The world-wide parrot fishes or rainbow fishes belong to these two families very near to the *Labridae* (wrasse). Having seen them in the West Indies, Ceylon, Bali, Hawaii and elsewhere, I can only admire the genius who has called them rainbow fishes, for their variety of colour seems to be without end, and a glorious puzzle for the statistician. Their mouths and vivid and varied colouring have given them the other obvious name of parrot fish. Usually they are not considered good food, though in Hawaii the half brown, half white one is considered edible. I had no chance to cook them well, so I cannot confirm or deny. Both the *Sparisomidae* and the *Scaridae* have teeth fused into a solid beak instead of those like wrasse. Their scales are much heavier. The smaller ones are easy shots and are no fighters. They are better left decorating the reefs and nibbling at their molluscs or coral.

In the *Scaridae* family there are, surprisingly, two sporting parrot fishes. I was particularly struck with the strength of the large rainbow parrot fish. I have speared several in Bermuda, Jamaica and Haiti. This large, half-brown, half-green species is rather timid but even when hit fairly and squarely in a good spot it will tear off at tremendous speed. I have never held one of the bigger ones, that is, one over twenty kilogrammes, with only one hit. Once, years ago, in Jamaica I had to go up, put on an Aqualung, and go down again and start breaking off large chunks of coral to get at one that had hidden in a hole, having wrenched itself off my spear. After twenty minutes of hard work I realized that I would have to heave away the whole of this particular reef to get at the wounded fish, and reluctantly gave up my attempt. In Jamaica I also came across the large blue parrot or Clamacore feeding at noon in the middle of a little lagoon surrounded by corals. The lagoon looked like a crater and the edges of this apparent coral volcano were actually above the surface. I saw the parrot fishes feeding off seaweed and coral in such a way that their backs were, from time to time, out of the water. From far away and in the strong sunlight it seemed to me that this closely knit group of some twenty or thirty blue parrots was a stranded whale or manta ray. I had to climb over the reef edge and glide silently along in shallow water, tearing my chest on the coral, before I could get near enough to bag one.

Some species of parrot fish occasionally go as far north as New York. They have beautiful colours and are no doubt a great asset to the coral reefs. I must, however, admit that they look so stupid, and their eyes and mouths are so ugly, that I dislike them intensely. Having seen their cowardly behaviour and the unattractive mud-coloured jet they emit from their anal holes when they dash off in fright, I must place them among the less appealing fish. One species in the Mediterranean has the descriptive name *Cretensis*. Though this refers to the island of Crete where this species was first identified, the French word, *cretin*, a congenital idiot, seems to be a happy play on words here.

Sheepshead porgy

PORGIES, SEA BREAMS or SCUPS. Family *Sparidae*
Found rather deeper than the grunts, these fish are the Atlantic equivalent of the Mediterranean sea breams, and particularly the striped sea bream. Usually quite small, though some species attain one kilogramme. Their habitat is the Atlantic and the Caribbean. Usually much livelier and more difficult to spear than their Mediterranean cousins.

PUFFER or PORCUPINE FISHES. Family *Diodontidae*
When they fear an attack they raise the spines which cover their body and puff themselves up to twice their size so that they look almost spherical. The teeth in each jaw are fused into one unit, forming a powerful beak. I once put my finger into the mouth of one that had been speared an hour before and was thought dead. I shouted with pain while friends spent an agonizing minute trying to pry open the beak. Considered poisonous, but I was served one raw in Japan and as I was a guest I had to eat it. It was cut in thin slices like smoked salmon and with the sauce I was given, the fish was delicious.

SALMON and TROUT. Family *Salmonidae*
I hardly dare mention these in a book of this kind. The salmon and trout fishing traditions in the United States and Northern Europe are so strong that I feel spearfishermen would not be welcome in salmon and trout waters. At all events, spearing salmon and trout is unthinkable except by special permission and in certain rivers. Most of these would be too cold except for the hardy. Possibly

some species of so-called cannibal trout might be considered fair game. I have yet to hear of any serious effort by anyone caddish enough to spear salmon before they enter rivers in large schools. Commercial interests may have something to say here too.

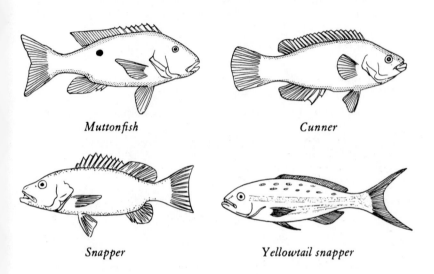

Muttonfish   *Cunner*

Snapper   *Yellowtail snapper*

SNAPPERS. Family *Lutianidae*.

The body is not too robust except in the larger red snapper. A family with many genera identified. Valued as food, some attain great size, and in particular the red or dog snapper (Pargo Colorado in Spanish speaking Central America). They live around shallow rocks, in wrecks and must be stalked in and around reefs, the spearfisherman relying on surprise appearances around corners. The best eating however is the muttonfish, recognized by a black spot, the size of a five pence piece or an American quarter, on each side of a pink body. The muttonfish, usually rather bigger than the smaller snappers, will keep just off a reef. It cruises about along the edge and when frightened will escape over the sands. Soon it will come back. I am afraid that more often than not I have to have two shots at a muttonfish. The first one is usually in hot pursuit away from the reef before the fish has got up speed. This means that it is hit from the back and a little from above. Very often a shot in the belly results and the muttonfish will tear itself off. It will go straight back to the reef and cower in the first hole it can find.

This gives me time for a careful shot in the head or gills which usually kills it quickly. In places where they are wary they are the best possible sport because they have learned to keep their distance and have learned the difference between a loaded and an unloaded gun. I once speared a red or dog snapper in the Bahamas and, having landed it in the approved manner for claiming world records, found it weighed 31·8 kilogrammes. I claimed a world record but the American authority, established for such recognition, decided it belonged to a sub-species of which I had no knowledge and for which a slightly bigger fish had been registered as a world record. Thus a chance for immortality eluded me.

Another well-known snapper is the schoolmaster, orange to yellow in colour, with white vertical lines. A harmless drudge. More exciting than the schoolmaster is the yellowtail snapper, a difficult fish to spear. Both are abundant over the coral reefs.

Squirrel fish

SQUIRREL or SOLDIER FISHES. Family *Holocentridae*
Bright pink, usually found in rocks, rather small, with large eyes, attains thirty centimetres. Good eating, especially smoked. Only absolute beginners should be allowed to shoot. Generally only south of Florida, but abundant in the Tropics, especially in the Pacific.

STURGEONS
Sturgeons belong to the SUBCLASS *Palaeopterygii* and not to the SUBCLASS *Neopterygii* to which bony fishes belong. In the United States they are now more or less extinct, but what a prize for a spearfisherman who lands one! Nobody knows how they would behave if they saw one of us under water. I doubt that the Russians or Iranians would allow us to try and spear sturgeons in the Caspian sea, even if we guaranteed to stalk only males. The caviar is too precious.

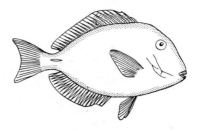

Ocean tang

SURGEON or DOCTORFISHES. Family *Acanthuridae*

Surgeonfishes, doctorfishes, unicorn fishes or tang are the names given to this family. Body moderately long, size up to thirty centimetres maximum. Although primarily inhabitants of the reefs, they also live in colder climates. Generally dull colours but quite attractive looking. Very good as food. At the base of the tail there are, on most of these, one or more bony spines. For their venomous qualities, see Chapter 6. Occasionally to be found further north than Florida. Beginners only, please.

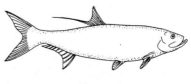

Tarpon

TARPONS. Family *Megalopidae*

The famous Atlantic tarpon is really a great prize for the spearfisherman. The adults often stay near the shore long enough for spearfishermen to have a chance to corner them. The young are very like the Mediterranean bass or sea wolf in behaviour. I have come suddenly upon five or six large ones all together in a quiet pool. There may have been some fresh water in the pools. Only quick action can be successful. They fight hard and the large and very shiny silver scales leave silver stains all over spearfishermen's bodies during the battle. The ageing Mussolini, with his lower jaw jutting heavily, looked like a tarpon. Their scales, especially of fully grown specimens, are so thick and strong that only a well-taken shot with a compressed-air gun from quite near will penetrate.

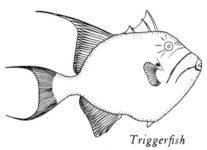

Triggerfish

TRIGGERFISHES. Family *Balistidae*

Triggerfishes are so called because of the first spine of the dorsal fin which can be locked erect. Found in all warm seas, they are called 'curious and degenerate' by Dr Smith. Powerful teeth crush all sorts of organisms for food. The body is encased in a heavy armour of leathery skin. Flesh considered poisonous, though many eat them with impunity. In Bermuda they are also called bastard turbot. The family belongs to the order of *Balistoidea*, where the names of other families indicate their similarity—filefishes, leather jackets, scrapers. Used as bait and not as food by anglers.

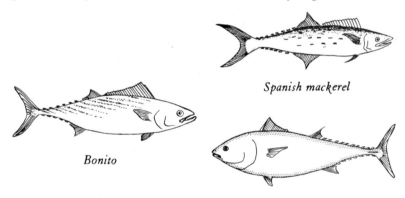

Spanish mackerel

Bonito

Bluefin tuna

TUNA and MACKEREL. Families *Scombridae* and
Scomberomonidae

Tuna (or, under its English name, tunny), bonito, albacore, mackerel, and wahoo, all famous game fishes, belong to these two families. Characteristic torpedo-shaped body, usually a metallic blue. Very small scales, dorsal fins in several parts as well as small fins behind anal fin. They also have one or more keels at the base of the caudal fin. They are found everywhere but in the coldest waters and, of course, some of the finest game fishes in the world belong to this family. There are certain places in the Mediterranean where tuna can be relied upon to pass year after year. The Greek coast facing west and, further north, the Jugoslav coast, are visited in September. The tuna always go the same way, with their right sides to the rough coast, and if there is the chance of a sandy coast appearing on either side, or a rough coast on the left, they go out to sea. I have, upon inquiry, admittedly not very thorough, found that their habit of keeping their right sides to a rocky coast is maintained in other seas. Aristotle, whose interest in the world below the water I have already mentioned in Chapter 1, even put forward the view that a tuna was blind in the left eye. I can certainly record that bonito and Spanish mackerel are not, as I have often met these fish and have been inspected by their left eyes.

While most of the tuna travel large distances in schools, I have always come upon single Spanish mackerel and bonito in small but not cohesive groups. They all have firm muscles and are beautifully built for speed. A tuna of fifty kilogrammes or over is a lost tuna if speared without having the line fixed to a Mae West or buoy. Mackerel will fight hard and usually go round in small circles in an attempt to get away. Most of the successful shots I have had at mackerel came after diving vertically down regardless of its circling, until I was deep enough to make a horizontal shot. To spear a mackerel with a handspear I consider the best sport under water.

Hogfish   *California sheepshead*

WRASSE. Family *Labridae*

The Mediterranean variety has been described. There is in the Western Hemisphere one famous species—the hogfish, which is excellent eating and which is, because of its timidity, good sport for the beginner spearfisherman. There are wrasse along the East Coast of the United States, while tropical waters are the habitat of the hogfish, tautog and cunner. The California sheepshead is the best-known wrasse on the West Coast.

GENERAL LIST

OCTOPUS. *Octopus*

Although not a fish, its fame demands a place here. Described in the Mediterranean list.

Captain Cousteau is the man who has dealt the death blow to the reputation of the poor octopus. The only big one he has ever seen attacking a man was a rubber one in a Hollywood picture. It is true, however, that Sir Arthur Grimble and others have seen large ones in the Pacific. Sir Arthur, in his famous book *A Pattern of Islands*, describes two men hunting a large octopus. One man dives and, pretending to be a helpless body, allows himself to be completely enveloped by the animal. His friend then dives and calmly bites the busy octopus between the eyes, and that is that.

The ordinary spearfisherman will not see such large ones unless he is very lucky. Even these are not likely to attack a man unless provoked. As long as the tentacles are not longer than your arm no possible harm can come to you while handling an octopus. If you see one, pick him up with your hand. Keep the tentacles off your face and neck and calmly bring him up in your hand. If he should grip you round your neck, do not get frightened. You are much stronger and you can pull one tentacle off easily and keep the others away from your face thereafter.

RAYS. ORDER *Rajae* of the CLASS of *Cartilaginous* fishes

Some genera of this great ORDER are described in the Mediterranean list (as is the way to spear them), but in the Western Hemisphere and other tropical seas they occur in great numbers. Sizes go up to several hundred kilogrammes and the families worth drawing attention to are: The sand or shovelnose sharks or guitarfishes (*Rhinobatidae*) which, in spite of their names belong to the ray ORDER (I saw a giant one in Madagascar at least six metres long); the whipless rays or skates (*Rajidae*); the eagle or bullrays (*Aetobatidae*), sometimes also called marble, leopard or spotted rays.

Then follow the straight stingrays (*Dasyatidae*), the mantas, devil-fishes or devilrays or mantas (*Mobulidae*) which Dr Hans Hass has seen in the Red Sea up to two or three tons in weight, chiefly distinguished by a fleshy projection on each side of the mouth. Lastly there are the electric rays (*Torpedinidae*).

The stingrays will not normally attack the human being. Here I repeat that the spearfisherman who can see under water will have the advantage over other swimmers because he will avoid stepping on a ray partly covered by sand. The big ones are a marvellous sight cruising about and moving slowly and gracefully like some animate delta-winged aircraft out of a children's book. The speckled, leopard, eagle or marble rays are particularly beautiful. I refer to the venomous whip-like dart in Chapter VI.

If you must spear one, approach it horizontally from the side, spear it in the eye and then hold on. Perhaps the best way of spearing it is towards the tip of the wing, which prevents free motion. I learned this from Dr Bruno Vailati, the famous Italian explorer, spearfisherman and leader of the Italian Red Sea Expedition in 1953. Get out of the water before you try to take the fish off your spear. You cannot do this in the water and keep far enough away to avoid being struck by its spine. See the Mediterranean list for removing the spine.

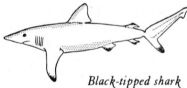

Black-tipped shark

SHARKS

We know almost nothing of sharks. The legends about them and the true accounts of their ferocity all stem from the experiences of people with their heads in the air, i.e. men in boats, ordinary swimmers and shipwrecked seamen. It seems, now that we have begun to assemble information from men who are themselves under the water at the time of meeting sharks, that we shall have to revise much of our thinking about them.

At the time of rewriting this book I have come up against over two hundred and sixty sharks at close quarters under water. From this experience all over the world I can draw no final conclusions except, perhaps, that sharks do not attack on sight each time they see a human being under water. I have questioned very

closely some of the most celebrated men of the spearfishing world
and not one of them (and this adds up to many hundreds of cases
of meeting sharks under water), has ever been wounded by a shark.
To give the reader an idea of the areas covered, my questions were
addressed to Hans Hass on his experiences in the Mediterranean,
the Red Sea and the Caribbean and also off the Great Barrier Reef,
to Bruno Vailati in the Red Sea, to Rodney Jonklaas in the waters
off Ceylon, to Renzo Avanzo in Sicily, the Italian Mediterranean
coast and the Red Sea, to Don Clark in California and Tahiti and to
Jack Ackerman whose life is in the waters of the Hawaiian Islands.
The famous French spearfisherman Marcel Isy-Schwart, gives a
lucid and intelligent account of his experiences off the Brazilian
coast in *Chasses aux Fauves de la Mer*, Horay, Paris, 1953. Gustav
DallaValle has written of his experiences with sharks in Haitian
waters. The Italian magazine *Mondo Sommerso* and the Californian
magazine *Skin Diver* are also reliable repositories of information
on sharks. My own experience covers most of the world, but in
waters close to the shore. There have been many books on sharks,
most of them legend spreading. Exceptions are *Shark Attack* by
V. M. Coppelson, Angus and Robertson, London 1962, and *Sharks
and Survival*, edited by P. W. Gilbert with the co-operation of the
Shark Research Panel of the American Institute of Biological
Sciences, D. C. Heath and Co., Boston 1963.

All the sharks met have been encountered in relatively shallow
water near the shore or near reefs which are high enough to form
islands. We have had little experience of sharks in the open sea.

As long as the spearfisherman was swimming along the surface
to all intents and purposes looking like a big fish approximately
two metres long, or if he was cruising below the surface with an
Aqualung, he was left completely alone. Sometimes the sharks
paid absolutely no attention and simply passed by. This was more
likely if the spearfisherman carried a loaded gun or handspear.
Sometimes they circled menacingly and both Hass and Isy-Schwart
have had the unenviable experience of being in fact the object
towards which a shark has lunged as though in attack. Each shouted,
the one in the Mediterranean, the other off the Brazilian coast, and
miraculously the sharks stopped in their tracks, turned and
disappeared into the blue. The same thing happened to Hass again
in Australia with a hammerhead shark, in full view of dozens of
people on a pier. This time Hass did not shout, but for some reason

the hammerhead behaved as though he had been hit by a whip and disappeared. Once, early on in the game, Isy-Schwart fired a pathetically inadequate harpoon straight at what he thought was an attacking shark. The spear, of course, simply bounced off but the shark turned and disappeared in apparently reckless flight. Captain Cousteau's celebrated blow on a shark's nose with his camera is known all over the world. I have hit dozens of sharks but they did not fight back, and I have landed only nine sharks in all these years.

Once off Haiti I lay in wait in one metre of water for a shark that I saw approaching over a coral reef barely sixty centimetres under water. My intention was to hit it from below, just behind the mouth. This meant waiting until the shark was two metres off, lowering myself gently down and holding on to coral with my left hand. I wanted to hold on without breathing, hoping that the shark would pass over me. Just as I was about to fire, the coral rock which I was holding to prevent myself from floating up broke with a loud smack and the shark flew off with what appeared to me the speed of sound. It did in fact pass straight over me, but I never had a chance to fire.

Rodney Jonklaas only once thought a shark was going for him, but he was relieved to find that it was attacking the string of fish he had speared and was dragging behind him. I once speared a jack in Fiji. Before I knew what was happening, a shark appeared from nowhere from behind me and snatched the struggling fish. I was so surprised that I had my handspear and fish ripped out of my hand and the shark disappeared into the blue, leaving me alone, embarrassed and with empty hands.

Don Clark, a prominent member of the Bottom Scratchers Club of La Jolla in California has described to me his experiences in Tahiti. He has had much experience with sharks and it is worth quoting his own words from an article in Skin Diver. 'When you spear a fish and see the sharks rushing in before you can pull it in to you, let the fish go, let them have it and yell under water or hit the surface, then swim slowly to your canoe or the shallow water. But if you have already pulled the fish in to you when the sharks come streaking in, then to protect your own hide as well as the fish, hold it tightly in your arms to prevent it from struggling, and turn your back on the sharks.'

Frankly, I am scared when I have to turn my back on them and keep corkscrewing my neck, while some of my pearl-diver friends remain perfectly calm and ignore the sharks—even those who have been badly bitten! They come in slowly on the blood scent of a speared fish, but a lot of blood would bring them fast.

I once speared a small hornback shark off the Coronado Islands and I hit it in the gills. It would appear that the shark is asphyxiated if his gills are pierced and will not fight much if properly hit there. This is also the experience of many others. My own triumph was short lived, because when I returned with my hornback to the landing barge of the US Navy Underwater Demolition Team, whose guest I was, I found a bigger one already there. I asked the sailors who had got that one. 'The General did,' they replied. The General in question was Major-General Greatsinger Farrell, US Marine Corps, Retired, who at fifty-seven still spearfished, having been one of the world's pioneers in our sport in the twenties.

'Where did the General hit his?' I asked.

'He didn't hit it,' was the reply. 'He pulled it out by the tail.'

I wondered what it must be like facing young and active US Marines in battle when their retired generals do this sort of thing.

Sharks are apt to appear from nowhere if a speared fish is allowed to splash about at or below the surface. At first we did not know if it was the vibrations of the wriggling fish that had attracted them or the smell of blood. It is impossible to believe that a little blood spilled could be detected by sharks at great distances so quickly, blessed though they may be by a highly sensitive nose. It is more likely to be the vibrations caused by a fish in trouble that attracts them as I have suggested earlier.

The members of the great Italian Underwater Expedition to the Red Sea in 1953 found that sharks approached them as soon as their heads were out of the water and Cousteau and I have found them much more timid in the depths. I have hit many sharks and failed to pierce their bodies. They invariably immediately disappeared in fear. Polynesian pearl divers are not troubled by sharks when they are below the surface, but they have found it worthwhile to develop a system by which two men in a boat pull a man out with lightning speed as he breaks surface. One of the few authenticated cases of a diver being so bitten by a shark was reported to me by the Italian Expedition. A native of the Red Sea had his leg bitten off while getting into a boat.

Yet, as we all know, so many people, while bathing, have been 'taken away' (as they say in Australia) by sharks. The history of navigation is strewn with cases of men being eaten by sharks and expecially on the high seas at night. It is dangerous to be definite because we have so little experience, but for the moment, and only provisionally, I would hazard this advice.

If you are under water and you have no speared fish about you and you meet a shark, swim on as quietly as you can, do not make any hurried movements. Keep your arms to your body and move your feet slowly and smoothly. Pretend you are a big fish. Swim quietly away and try to prevent your heart bursting through your ribs. You have an excellent chance of coming out alive. In any case, the shark may be one of a type variously named nurse shark, sand shark or basking shark, with no teeth and only interested in plankton as food.

If you are like Jonklaas and Don Clark and insist on dragging speared fish with you in shark-infested waters, then you would not need or heed any advice from me anyway.

At all events, we who can see under the water have a tremendous advantage over the poor wretch who swims about with his head in the fool's paradise of air and sunshine while the rest of his body is exposed, defenceless and alluring, to the sharks below.

At least we spearfishermen can, like Hass, myself and the others, see the shark in time, shout at it, even fire a spear at it, and thus perhaps earn a reprieve we might not have had as an ordinary bather, or floating about with a safety belt around us. I should like to see ships' life boats and aircraft supplied with masks, fins and floating rubber mattresses in addition to safety belts. The only case of a spearfisherman, behaving as I have advised, being attacked by a shark, with no provocation of speared fish near him is Rodney Fox in South Australia. He was bitten by a great white shark (*Charcharodon charcharias*). He survived by hitting the shark with his spear and swimming half a mile back for shore, bleeding profusely. The shark, having let go, never returned.

At some stage in the middle of World War II and in the course of a session of the House of Commons, a Member of Parliament pointed out that there was a plague of sharks off the East Coast of England, and asked what the Government was going to do about it. Sir (then Mr) Winston Churchill replied that he needed notice of the question, but in the meantime assured the Hon Member that HM Government were absolutely opposed to sharks. I dare say that, had spearfishing been invented when he was much younger, Sir Winston would have been prepared to oppose them personally under water. The beginner at spearfishing should not try to do any such thing. The skin of most sharks is hard enough to prevent mortal blows by a spear and a wounded shark may not always run for dear life. If you must shoot at a shark, wait till you are sure you cannot miss getting a spear in its gills, but do not do this unless you or one or two companions have other spears ready to be fired in the other gill or at the brain or the softer underside. The position of the brain varies so you would have to know your shark before firing at the brain. The bone-hard cartilage which protects the shark's brain once bent my spear point to ninety degrees without being pierced more than very little. They belong to the CLASS of cartilaginous fishes of which there is a SUBCLASS *Euselachii* to which both sharks and rays belong. Information about sharks is still vague, but it appears that for thousands of years they have been so superior to their environment that many species have changed little over the ages. We may be dealing with creatures of a mentality quite incomprehensible to Man who is used to modern animals. It is thus dangerous to generalize about sharks. Classification is bound to undergo drastic changes when we learn more. Sometimes only adults are known, sometimes juveniles of unknown adults. Gill openings are separate, slitlike. A greatly developed sense of smell and sensitivity to vibrations aids them to find their prey. I have already said that I have known them to appear out of nowhere when a fish has been speared. No ordinary scales or skin. The best-known names for shark are port jackson, blackfin, great white, black, brown, blue, bluefin, nurse, sand, basking, thresher, man-eater, porbeagle, tiger, whale, mako, and, of course, the peculiar-looking hammerhead. The names of nurse, sand, basking, and whale shark are given to the varieties that are sluggish and that are not carnivorous.

Off the coasts of the British Isles and the United States and in many other seas there are to be found many kinds of dogfish and catfish, minor and more sluggish sharks. By behaving quietly you may easily succeed in getting them within firing distance. A shot in the gills is a telling blow, and provided it has penetrated deep enough, you will have the pleasure of being able to boast of having landed a shark after all.

A golden sea bream, one of the best eating fishes. The photo illustrates a full wet suit, a compressed-air gun with short line, a rather long line snorkel and a full face mask. Photograph by Roberto Dei

SEALS, SEA LIONS, DOLPHINS, WHALES

Off the Coronado Islands near the California-Mexico border I swam about among California sea lions of all sizes. They were extremely curious and dived all round me but never made any attempt to attack. I feel sure that a mother would attack me if I tried to go for her young. I do not believe that any of these mammals would attack a fellow mammal out spearfishing except in self-defence. It is said that killer whales attack unprovoked, but they are almost never seen near the shore. I once saw one as it passed quite near me in the British Virgin Islands some miles off shore while diving at a thirty-metre-deep reef. It paid no attention to me.

TURTLES

I have caught many turtles under water with my hands. Their natural means of defence have not protected them from being caught by us holding their dorsal shell on both sides so that our hands could be reached by their beaks. If you hold the turtle's shell so that its head is pointed upwards, you will be pulled upwards. The bigger the turtle, the quicker will you be brought to the surface. Even the biggest turtles fly when pursued. I once landed one of forty kilogrammes this way. This one proved to be excellent eating, but it is advisable to follow local advice because there are many cases of poisoning through eating turtle flesh.

LARGE GAME FISHES

The various marlins, sailfishes, wahoo, swordfishes, large tarpons, tuna and the pelagic sharks are big game by any man's reckoning. I look to the day when the more adventurous spearfishermen will go forth to the high seas and, equipped with adequate gear for holding on to these big fish, will try to spear them. As things are today, a really big pelagic specimen of any of the above will simply take the spearfisherman with it.

INDEX